DISCARDED

D0263946

Plot summary

1 Act 1: April 1912. Brumley, a Midlands town. The Birling family and Gerald Croft are enjoying a dinner to celebrate Sheila's engagement to Gerald.

4 At this moment the doorbell rings. They are not expecting a visitor. The maid announces that an Inspector has arrived.

2 Arthur Birling, Sheila's father, is particularly pleased, since the marriage should mean closer links with a rival company run by Gerald's father. He is optimistic about life in England — he sees peace, prosperity and progress.

3 When the ladies leave the room, Birling lectures both his son Eric and Gerald about the importance of every man looking out for himself if he wants to get on in life.

10 Sheila gives the engagement ring back to Gerald.

11 The Inspector turns his attention to Mrs Sybil Birling, who confesses that she also had contact with Eva, but not under that name.

12 Eva, desperate and pregnant, approached a charity chaired by Mrs Birling to ask for help. Help was refused because Sybil was offended by the girl calling herself 'Mrs Birling'. She says that the baby's father should be made entirely responsible.

17 The phone rings. A girl has just died on her way to the infirmary. A police officer is coming to question them!

16 Arthur, Sybil and Gerald congratulate themselves that it was all a hoax and that they can carry on as before. This attitude upsets Sheila and Eric.

5 Inspector Goole says that he is investigating the death of a young woman, Eva Smith.

6 Birling is shown a photograph of Eva. He then remembers that he sacked her in 1910 for leading a pay strike. He feels justified in this action.

7 The investigation moves on to Sheila. Sheila also had Eva sacked by complaining about her manner when served by her in a department store. Sheila regrets this.

8 The Inspector says that Eva changed her name to Daisy Renton. Gerald acts guiltily.

9 Act 2: Gerald explains that he had an affair with Eva, but has not seen her since he ended it in Autumn 1911.

13 Act 3: Eric is revealed as the father. He has stolen money from Birling's office to help Eva. Eric turns on his mother when he learns that she has refused to help.

14 The Inspector tells them they are all partly to blame for Eva's death and warns them of the consequences of people not being responsible for each other.

15 After he leaves, the family begin to suspect that the Inspector was not a genuine police officer. A phone call to the Chief Constable confirms this. They phone the infirmary to discover that no suicide case has been brought in that day.

Arthur Birling

Mr Birling is upper middle class, a successful <u>factory owner</u>, <u>ex-Lord</u> <u>Mayor</u> of Brumley and a <u>local magistrate</u>. He <u>regards</u> <u>himself</u> <u>as</u> <u>reasonable</u> and pays his employees no more and no less than the going rate. He feels that it is his <u>duty</u> to keep costs low and prices high.

Birling has <u>little</u> <u>or</u> <u>no</u> <u>imagination</u>, and <u>seems</u> <u>blind</u> both to the consequences of his own actions, and to events in the larger world. He makes predictions about the future – the unsinkability of *The Titanic*; the impossibility of war; the promise of technology – which would have been believed by many in 1912, but which would have seemed <u>laughably</u> <u>optimistic</u> and <u>shortsighted</u> to audiences in 1945, who knew what really happened. Birling is a <u>stereotype</u> for his time in many ways, and this is also true of other characters in the play. He is a <u>caricature</u> of the callous heartlessness of a <u>capitalistic</u> <u>businessman</u>.

Birling is self-centred and <u>proud</u> <u>of</u> <u>his</u> <u>status</u>. He sets great store by his <u>public</u> <u>offices</u> and privileges and tries, initially, to put the Inspector in his place by emphasising his own position in society. So sensitive is he about such matters that he even feels a little uneasy about Gerald Croft marrying his daughter, sensing that Gerald's titled parents may feel that their son is marrying 'beneath himself'. At the end of the play, the possibility that he may be deprived of his promised knighthood upsets him far more than anything else.

Birling has been an <u>indulgent</u> <u>parent</u>, but he has not prepared Eric to face the realities of life. As Eric says, 'you're not the kind of father a chap could go to when he's in trouble'. Birling has paid for Eric's expensive education, largely, one suspects, because that displays his wealth and enhances his own social status. In Act 3 it is plain that Birling's motives are not to save Eric from being found out, but to <u>protect</u> <u>himself</u> from social scandal. To do this he is prepared to distort or ignore the truth. He is blind to this <u>hypocrisy</u>, and indifferent when it is pointed out. Just before the end of the play he happily argues that <u>'the</u> <u>whole</u> <u>thing's</u> <u>different</u> <u>now'</u>, and congratulates himself on having avoided a scandal. Provided his public reputation is safe, Birling will never change.

Sybil Birling

Mrs Birling is even more hard-faced and <u>arrogant</u> than her husband. She is introduced as his social superior and her manner indicates that she is very <u>conscious</u> <u>of</u> <u>social</u> <u>position</u>, especially her own. She is extremely <u>snobbish</u>, and expects others to show her respect and defer to her opinions. She resents being contradicted, even when caught by the Inspector telling outright lies.

Mrs Birling seems genuinely shocked to hear about her son's drink problem, although the information does not surprise Sheila or Gerald. Her concern that Sheila should not be exposed to 'unpleasant' things suggests that she regards her daughter as a child. Is Mrs Birling <u>genuinely</u> <u>unaware</u> of what is going on around her, or is she <u>deliberately</u> <u>blind</u> to anything she does not wish to see?

When exposed to criticism, Mrs Birling retreats behind words like <u>'respectable'</u>, <u>'duty'</u> and <u>'deserving'</u>. If she feels her own status has been suitably acknowledged, she will be condescendingly generous, but if not, she will take offence at what she sees as 'impertinence'. She thinks that people from the <u>'lower</u> <u>classes'</u> are almost a <u>different</u> <u>species</u>. Eva Smith's pleas for help offend Mrs Birling, because the girl was 'giving herself ridiculous airs' and 'claiming elaborate fine feelings'. Her <u>vindictive</u> attitude towards the father of the girl's child changes dramatically when she learns that he is her own son, clearly illustrating her extreme hypocrisy.

Mrs Birling tries to use her husband's social position to intimidate the Inspector, and is confused when this tactic fails. She argues that if she had been present when the Inspector first arrived, she would have stood up to him.

At the end of the play Mrs Birling has not allowed herself to learn anything that will make her behave in a compassionate or caring way in the future. Perhaps the Inspector's call has only served to harden her attitudes.

Sheila Birling

Sheila, the Birlings' daughter, is impressionable, and is deeply affected by the Inspector's revelations. She and her brother Eric are the only characters who give any cause for optimism in the play. Sheila has an attractive and essentially honest character, and lacks the cold-blooded attitude of her parents.

Sheila seems at times almost to be an accomplice of the Inspector in that she tends to take up his criticism of the other characters, becoming his mouthpiece when he has left the stage. Her parents see this as disloyalty, Gerald sees vindictiveness, but Sheila realises that there is no point in concealing the truth – it is time to abandon all pretences. She objects to her parents' attempts to protect her from unpleasant truths. Until the arrival of the Inspector, Sheila has been content with the socially acceptable hypocrisy about such things, but Inspector Goole's revelations about her family are a learning experience for her.

Because she is more sensitive than the others, Sheila is the first to realise what the Inspector is driving at in his interviews with herself and the others. She sees through the other characters' attempts to cover the truth. She is aware that the Inspector knows all about them and is the first to wonder who the Inspector really is.

Although Sheila identifies with the dead girl, her <u>spiteful</u> <u>complaint</u> against Eva is probably the most indefensible action of all, as it is based merely on her own wounded vanity. However, she felt bad about it at the time, regretted it deeply later, and is honest enough to admit her share of the responsibility for Eva's suicide.

Sheila and her brother Eric represent the <u>younger</u> <u>generation</u> that Priestley hopes is still open-minded enough to learn to accept responsibility for others.

Gerald Croft

Gerald is the <u>upper</u> <u>class</u> fiancé of Sheila Birling, and the son of Arthur Birling's business rival, Sir George Croft. Although he is only aged about 30, Gerald's <u>outlook</u> <u>on</u> <u>life</u> <u>is</u> <u>similar</u> <u>to</u> <u>that</u> <u>of</u> <u>Mr</u> <u>Birling</u>. He agrees with the way Birling handled Eva Smith's dismissal. Like Mr and Mrs Birling, Gerald's first impulse is to <u>conceal</u> his involvement with Eva; but unlike them, he shows <u>genuine</u> <u>remorse</u> when the news of her death finally sinks in. Moreover, it becomes clear that Gerald helped Eva out of <u>genuine</u> <u>sympathy</u> for her situation and did not take advantage of her in the violent and drunken way in which Eric did. Gerald did make Eva genuinely happy for a time, and in many ways is the least to blame for her death. He makes it clear that both he and Eva understood that the relationship was to be a short-term affair. Nevertheless, *he* was the one <u>in</u> <u>control</u> of the timing of events.

At the end of the play, Gerald shows the <u>clearest</u> <u>head</u> in thinking about the identity of the Inspector, is the first to begin devising a way out, and shows <u>initiative</u> in telephoning the infirmary to check if a dead girl has actually been admitted. He also suggests the possibility of there being more than one girl involved.

Gerald seems to have abandoned his genuine remorse by the end of the play. He expects Sheila to accept the engagement ring again and asserts that all is now well.

Eric Birling

Eric, the Birlings' son, is, like Sheila, in his early twenties, but is probably the younger of the two, judging by his less mature attitude. During the play, he is exposed as a drunkard, the father of an illegitimate unborn child, a liar and a thief. During the first two Acts, Eric functions mainly as an irritant to Mr Birling's complacency, continually asking questions that his father regards as silly. Mr Birling clearly thinks that his son has not benefited from his expensive education.

Eric arouses curiosity with his sudden guffaw in Act 1. This is possibly an indication that he knows something about Gerald's neglect of Sheila. Curiosity about him turns to suspicion when he breaks off in mid-comment. We begin to think that Eric has something to conceal.

Eric seems hostile towards his parents, especially his father, whom he finds unapproachable and unloving. This may be why Eva treated Eric as if he were a 'kid' and why he responded to her pity. She may have recognised in him a need for affection which she herself shared.

Eric may be a weak and lonely figure, but he is capable of real feeling for others. He is more demonstrative than the others, and at the end he is on the verge of physically attacking his mother in fury at her lack of charity. In his eyes, his mother 'murdered' his child and its mother, but remember also that Eric's share of responsibility for Eva's suicide is very great. Eric has definitely learned something from the evening's revelations and may now be more than a 'silly boy'.

Inspector Goole

The Inspector is an enigmatic figure. He neither changes nor develops, but frequently repeats: 'I haven't much time', as if he is working to a pre-arranged schedule.

Inspector Goole's name is an obvious pun on 'ghoul', a malevolent spirit or ghost. He could be seen as some kind of spirit, sent on behalf of the dead girl to torment the consciences of the characters in the play, or as a sort of cosmic policeman conducting an inquiry as a preliminary to the Day of Judgement, or simply as a forewarning of things to come. Certainly it seems that Priestley did not want to promote a single interpretation of who the Inspector 'really' is. The character's dramatic power lies in this. To have revealed his identity as a hoaxer or as some kind of 'spirit' would have spoilt the unresolved tension that is so effective at the end of the play.

The stage directions for the Inspector stress his purposefulness and deliberate manner of addressing people. There is an air of menace about him and, unlike all the other characters, he does not deviate from his moral position. He is single-minded in pursuing his chosen line of investigation. He alone is certain of his facts. These facts are questioned by the other characters only after he has left.

Goole makes judgements about characters which they feel are unusual and inappropriate in a police inspector. He undermines their complacent assumption that they are respectable citizens. Each of them finds this a shattering experience. Those characters who resist telling the Inspector the truth suffer more than those who are more open. The Inspector says to Gerald, 'if you're easy with me, I'm easy with you'. Notice that he makes no judgement upon Gerald, and deliberately tries to stop Sheila from blaming herself too much. However, he begins to lose patience with Mr Birling. Mrs Birling resists the truth the most, and the Inspector is accordingly harshest with her.

The Inspector persuades characters to reveal things which they would rather were not known. Sheila points out that there is something about the Inspector which makes them tell him things because they feel that he already knows.

Inspector Goole has several functions in the play. He acts as the storyteller, linking the separate incidents into one coherent life-story. He often supplies dates or fills in background information. He also behaves like a father confessor to each character, encouraging them to acknowledge their guilt for Eva's suicide and to repent. Significantly, the Inspector himself neither forgives nor punishes. Each character is made to face up to the fact that they must find the courage to judge themselves; only then will they have learned enough to be able to change.

Sometimes the Inspector behaves as the voice of social conscience. He points out that social responsibilities become greater as privileges increase. He also plays the traditional role of a policeman in a 'whodunnit' story, slowly uncovering the truth through careful questioning, piecing together evidence with shrewd insight, though in this case not one character has done anything to Eva Smith which a court of law would describe as a crime.

Is the Inspector's investigation successful? Eric and Sheila may have learned enough to change their ways, but the others, even at the end, strongly oppose such changes. Post-war audiences of 1945 would have appreciated the Inspector's prophecy of a lesson that 'will be taught…in fire and blood and anguish'.

Eva Smith

Eva Smith dominates the action invisibly. By the end of the play she is as familiar as the other characters. She is presented in an <u>idealised</u> way: she was very pretty, with large dark eyes and soft, brown hair. She was lively, intelligent and warm-hearted.

Eva is depicted as the <u>innocent victim</u> of selfishness. She was a <u>good worker</u>, but was sacked because of victimisation. She was abandoned by Gerald when she became inconvenient. She was a <u>compliant</u> outlet for Eric's sexual needs and loneliness, but was also made an accomplice to theft and made pregnant by him. She was discarded as unworthy of help when she did not pander to Mrs Birling's self-importance.

Each incident illustrates that Eva is <u>easy prey for 'respectable' society</u>. In spite of the way society treats her, she shows kindness and sensitivity beyond the reach of the others, as demonstrated particularly in her dealings with Eric. Although the victim of exploitation, she refuses to treat others as they have treated her, even though she is in a position to create scandal for them all. As Eva Smith's fortunes sink she is revealed as increasingly <u>noble</u>, the complete opposite to most of the other characters. There is an <u>affinity between Eva and Sheila</u>: they are the same age, and Sheila might have suffered the same fate as Eva had not luck given her a more privileged position in society. Eva Smith and 'John Smith' represent ordinary people who can be destroyed by indifference when society fails to grant them the right of basic human dignity.

Even if there was no single Eva Smith, as Gerald suggests, we can still see how complacency, selfishness and thoughtlessness can damage others.

About the author

> **J. B. Priestley *was in some ways the conscience of a nation*** (Tom Priestley, son)

J. B. Priestley 1940

John Boynton Priestley (1894–1984) was one of the most popular, versatile and prolific authors of his day. Though he may not have produced an unquestioned masterpiece, his work in many fields of literature and thought, written from the 1920s to his death, is still highly valued. The best-known of his 16 novels is *The Good Companions* (1929), which has since been adapted for stage, film and television.

It was as a playwright and a political and social thinker that J. B. Priestley was especially important, and certainly these two aspects are what matter most in our study of *An Inspector Calls*. He wrote some 40 plays, of which maybe eight are still performed with some regularity. There are two types of play for which he is especially remembered. One type is regional and nostalgic: plays set in his native Yorkshire at some time before the First World War. The most popular of these is undoubtedly the boisterous comedy, *When We Are Married* (1938). The second group are the so-called 'time plays', such as *Dangerous Corner* (1932), in which themes of fate, responsibility and personal choice are presented by the use of chronological devices.

Politically, J. B. Priestley was a patriotic socialist whose love of his country could appear nostalgic, but who was passionately convinced of the need for social change to benefit the poor. During the Second World War, his weekly broadcasts were highly influential and expressed his faith in the ordinary people of Britain. In the last year of the war Priestley was writing *An Inspector Calls*, which he saw as a contribution to public understanding that might lead to a Labour election victory after the war (as happened in 1945).

The drama unfolds in one place (the Birlings' dining room). The action is straightforward, without any complicating subplots, and the events depicted in the play actually take up about the same amount of time as that which passes in the theatre. The breaks between Acts are not allowed to disturb the action of the play, which makes it realistic and convincing, concentrates the attention of the audience, and makes the ending all the more startling.

Priestley has, therefore, closely observed the Three Unities of Classical Greek drama. The Unity of Place meant that the location of the action stayed the same. The Unity of Time originally meant that (as here) stage time and real time were identical. The Unity of Action indicated that there was only one main plot. This play is even short enough (about an hour and three-quarters) for some productions to play without an interval, thus increasing the sense of unity.

Everything that actually happened to Eva Smith is described or reported to us. All these events happen 'off stage'. In this sense, the Inspector acts like a Chorus in a Greek play. From time to time he sums up what has happened, comments on the characters, and explains to everyone the lessons to be learned. This includes the audience, who can see their own faults reflected in the play's characters. This was another very old dramatic tradition which was thought to make for a good play. Would it have made the play more or less effective if we had actually met Eva Smith, or actually seen the things which happened to her? In the 1953 film version we are shown all the encounters with Eva Smith in flashback. It is worth watching this film to answer the above question. Be aware of other changes to the script: Inspector Goole does not leave by the front door; like a spirit, he just disappears!

It is very easy just to see *An Inspector Calls* as a period piece set in 1912. There are many ways in which it resembles plays set in the North of England in late Victorian times or in the years before the First World War. For example, *Hobson's Choice* (written by Harold Brighouse in 1916, set in Salford in 1880) and Priestley's own *When We Are Married* (set in his birth-place of Bradford) deal with domineering businessmen and local politicians whose weaknesses and failings of character are exposed. These are both comedies; *An Inspector Calls* is not, but characters, settings and the use of dramatic revelations are similar.

An Inspector Calls is at least as much about 1945 as about 1912. Despite Mr Birling's smugness about the future, the history of Britain from 1912 onwards was far from trouble-free. The First World War began in 1914, to be followed by a time of severe industrial unrest – in 1926 there was a General Strike. There was mass unemployment in the Depression years, and the rise of Fascism brought international unrest and fear throughout the 1930s. The government was seen to be doing little about these problems, with Prime Minister Chamberlain's attempts to avoid war by negotiation with Hitler being particularly ineffective.

First World War soldiers

During the Second World War, many people became convinced that, after the great struggle against Fascism, we had to try to create a new fairer world in peacetime. J. B. Priestley's war-time broadcasts expressed this strongly, and so does *An Inspector Calls*. In fact these broadcasts were cancelled, in spite of their popularity, because Priestley was considered to be too critical of the government's policies. In the play he goes back to 1912 to show how a fair and just society depends upon compassion and responsibility for our fellow citizens. From 1945 to 1951 the new Labour government attempted to put this into practice. 1912 was superficially a time of great confidence, but the cracks were beginning to show. The end of an era was approaching.

An Inspector Calls can be seen as a sort of 'time play'. One advantage of this is a fairly straightforward use of hindsight. In particular, audiences at the end of the war must have appreciated the irony of Birling's predictions of peace and prosperity. His errors of judgement about technology and progress also serve to suggest that Birling is talking nonsense about other things, as when he says that a man has to look after himself and take no responsibility for others.

In considering *An Inspector Calls* as a 'time play', we should take note of Stephen Daldry's remarkable production, which made a supposedly 'old-fashioned' piece one of the most popular and thought-provoking plays of the 1990s. Rather than a realistic 1912-style dining room, the set was of a grand house in the middle of war-time destruction, positioned above the stage, rather like a doll's house, to symbolise the Birlings' detachment from social issues. Inspector Goole came from the 1940s world, giving yet another possible interpretation of him as a sort of 'Spirit of the Future', and remained on the street outside the house with the poor of the city. The world of the Birlings literally collapsed around them when the house toppled to the ground.

This staging emphasised that the play is not just about 1912, but about 1945 and even later. The production focused attention on the moral and political messages, not just the characters and story. In his highly detailed stage directions, Priestley acknowledges that 'an ordinary realistic set' is not the only option. Whatever the angle of the production, *An Inspector Calls* can still remain a highly effective thriller, a unique form of 'whodunnit'.

Status

Some characters in the play attach great importance to social status. For them, it is so precious that nothing must threaten it. Social class defines the value of human beings. A high social class insulates these characters from the unpleasantness of reality. Birling panics at the prospect of having his son's or his wife's actions made public. He is clearly terrified by a scandal which would irretrievably damage the Birlings' status. Eva Smith, who is working class, is seen by some characters, particularly upper middle class Mrs Birling, as having little value as a human being.

Social responsibility

The word 'responsibility', or variations on it, occurs frequently in the play. The play points out the need for a sense of personal responsibility in every member of society; responsibility not only for individual actions, but also for the way actions affect others. The Inspector voices these views most strongly, but is joined by Sheila and, to a lesser degree, Eric. In a sense, these characters act as the communal conscience of the other characters. The opposite view is expressed by Arthur Birling, whose driving concern is self-interest.

Guilt

The structure of *An Inspector Calls* is in many ways that of a 'whodunnit', and in such a crime story there must always be one – or more than one – guilty party. In this case (as in Agatha Christie's 1934 detective novel *Murder on the Orient Express*) all the 'suspects' are guilty, but of a social crime. They all, metaphorically, stab Eva Smith in the back. Different characters react to their guilt in different ways when it is revealed to them. Not all show remorse or shame, and some are so hardened that they refuse even to accept that remorse is appropriate. By the end of the play the characters have fallen into two groups: those who admit their wrongdoing and are likely to learn and change as a result of it, and those who are entrenched in their attitudes and appear to have learned no lasting lesson.

The characters must realise, accept and be responsible for the true results of what they have done if they are to recover their humanity. All the characters have something to lose by accepting their guilt and acting on it, and for some this is too high a price to pay.

Pride

The play also shows how true it is that pride comes before a fall – especially the false pride shown by some of the characters. Only by abandoning this pride can characters arrive at an honest relationship with themselves and each other. However some, notably Arthur and Sybil Birling, are unwilling to do this.

Lies

Lies abound in *An Inspector Calls*. Characters lie to each other, to the Inspector and to themselves. These lies are not confined to simple misrepresentations of the truth (as when Mrs Birling denies ever having met Eva Smith), some characters begin to see their whole lives as lies. The lies have formed the basis for their relationships with others – as in the case of Gerald and Sheila – and with themselves, and they see that they need to begin again, from a standpoint of truth. Other lies in the play concern the way people define things like 'respectability' or 'truth'. This kind of lie is what we normally refer to as 'hypocrisy'. A word often used in the play is 'pretence', which also draws attention to the theme of lying.

Text commentary

Act 1

Arthur Birling, a prosperous industrialist, holds a celebratory dinner to mark the engagement of his daughter Sheila to Gerald Croft (son of Sir George Croft, Birling's even more prosperous business rival). Birling toasts Sheila and Gerald. He says that this night is the happiest of his life, and looks forward to cooperation between his company and Sir George's.

> **"The dining-room of a fairly large suburban house"**

Explore

Pay attention to the scene and character directions. They are much more detailed than those supplied by most playwrights and can be very helpful when answering extract-based questions which demand a close analysis.

The entire play happens in this room, on one night during the first week of April in 1912. The room is 'substantial and heavily comfortable, but not cosy and homelike'. The Birling household is materially well-off, but only superficially happy and united.

Mr Birling is at pains to explain that the port is exactly the same as that bought by Gerald's father. Birling sees Sir George Croft as his social superior, and his comment about the port shows he is a <u>social</u> <u>climber</u>. He wishes to increase his <u>importance</u>, but does so by <u>going</u> <u>through</u> <u>the motions</u>, rather than doing anything really worthwhile. He may no longer be an alderman, or Lord Mayor, but he makes sure that everyone knows that he used to be, along with the facts that he is a local magistrate and a 'hard-headed', successful businessman.

Sheila introduces the first of several incidents which are at odds with the happy atmosphere. Gerald stayed away from her all the previous summer, although he says it was only because he was busy at the works. These incidents indicate that <u>unpleasantness may lurk beneath the surface</u> of the Birlings' apparently happy family life.

Sheila accuses her brother Eric of being somewhat drunk, or <u>'squiffy'</u>. This forewarns us about his <u>parents' ignorance</u> of his drinking habit. Mrs Birling's reaction shows her marked sense of propriety. Eric's reply and Sheila's comment suggest that there are things about both of them which their parents do not know.

Explore

'Squiffy' is popular slang of the early twentieth century. What other examples can you find in the text?

Sheila and Eric both use <u>slang</u> expressions which contrast with the language used by their parents. This helps to emphasise their <u>youth</u> and liveliness and contributes to the play's <u>authentic period atmosphere</u>. Each character uses <u>language</u> and speaks in a manner that helps to reveal his or her personality. Compare, for example, the pompous language of Birling with the clipped and incisive style of the Inspector, or the arch and stuffily condescending tone of Mrs Birling with Sheila's blunt and emotional manner. Such things not only affect the way we see each character, but also how we respond to what each says, how much weight we give it, and how far we are convinced by it.

> ❝ *You're just the kind of son-in-law I always wanted* ❞

Mr Birling is fairly ignorant of historical and political realities. All he can see is that he is a <u>successful businessman, alderman, friend to the Chief Constable, ex-Lord Mayor and past greeter of Royalty</u>, who is about to go up in the world. He is happy because Crofts Limited and Birling and Company may one day work together 'for lower costs and higher prices'. Birling seems to regard the marriage of his daughter almost as a commercial arrangement, and also as a way of increasing the family's social position, since Gerald is from a higher class.

> **I think it's perfect. Now I feel really engaged.**

Gerald gives Sheila a ring, which produces a **delighted** reaction. He offers it to her again at the end of the play, although her reaction then is very different to now. Sheila's comment that she will 'never let it go out of [her] sight for an instant' becomes ironic in the light of Gerald's revelations, which mean that she returns the ring to him within an hour of receiving it. For now, Sheila, the most **emotionally demonstrative** character in the play, shows her pleasure at the engagement ring by kissing Gerald.

It is interesting that Eric remarks upon Sheila's behaviour here, because he himself has an **explosive outburst of emotion** at the end of the play. The other characters are more restrained. Eric's comment, **'Steady the Buffs!'**, is a colloquialism.

> **Well, it came just at the right moment. That was clever of you, Gerald.**

Mrs Birling's admiration of Gerald's cleverness is **echoed** by her husband at the end of the play. There are many **parallels** like this in the play's construction, which help bind it together. The comment also fits in with the play's exploration of **timing** and its theme of **people manipulating others**. Remember that the Inspector is the master of timing.

> **I say there isn't a chance of war**

Mr Birling explains at length his uncomplicated idea of the world. His vision is **sunnily optimistic**. He dismisses the prospects of war, strikes and other problems in a **self-satisfied** way. The world is a **comfortable** place for Mr Birling: **'We're in for a time of steadily increasing prosperity'**. The Birling family is introduced as **confident**, united, assured, prosperous and self-righteous. Later in Act 1, much of this confidence is shown to be completely <u>unjustified</u>.

Mr Birling's trust in <u>technology</u> is illustrated by his reference to contemporary inventions and <u>'progress'</u>. However, it is shown that his optimism is no more 'unsinkable' than was *The Titanic*, which he mentions with such pride. Note that this speech places the action precisely in time. *The Titanic* sailed from Southampton on Tuesday 10th April 1912.

It is easy to laugh at Mr Birling with the benefit of <u>hindsight</u>. History tells us that his trust in the technology of 1912 is as sadly misplaced as is his assertion that there will never be another war. Birling's insistence here on the importance of 'facts' is <u>ironic</u> in the light of later events. He proves to be the most reluctant to face uncomfortable facts later in the play.

When the ladies leave the men to the port and cigars, as was the custom, they take Eric with them for a short while, leaving Mr Birling alone with Gerald: 'Eric – I want you a minute'. Note that we do not see Mrs Birling again until Act 2, which means that she is off stage for a considerable time. Think about why J. B. Priestley might have done this.

> **❝[Confidentially]** *By the way, there's something I'd like to mention* **❞**

Birling explains to Gerald how he understands Lady Croft's reported feelings concerning Sheila not being his social equal. Notice how this is something which Birling seems to take for granted, assuming that such concern should be <u>'only natural'</u> because of Lady Croft's background. What does this reveal about Birling's views on status and relationships?

Birling hints that he expects to get a knighthood, and that this may ease Lady Croft's concerns. He jokes that all should be well for his knighthood, so long as his family behaves itself and does not get into the police courts.

> **You seem to be a nice well behaved family**

Gerald's response (above) turns sour as the play proceeds, as attention becomes increasingly concentrated on much that **seems to be** pleasant and attractive. In all works of literature you should be alert to the word 'seems'. The **difference between appearance and reality** can be great.

Eric starts to say something but suddenly breaks off, becoming confused: **'Yes, I remember –'** Mr Birling and Gerald are faintly amused by this, and think it sounds as though he has been up to something. The audience's **curiosity** is also aroused. Later, it becomes clear that Eric's comment relates to his relationship with Eva Smith. Notice how Mr Birling's rather patronising remark about Eric, **'You don't know what some of these boys get up to nowadays'** is shown to be **ironic** in the light of later disclosures. The conversation between Birling and Gerald has been **man-to-man**. Eric has been described as only a **'boy'**. Birling remembers that when he was young, he and his friends were worked hard and kept short of cash, but **'we broke out and had a bit of fun sometimes'**. This, together with Gerald's reply, 'I'll bet you did', contains the suggestion that the 'fun' they had was with **women**. Given what is later revealed about Gerald's behaviour towards Eva, his innuendo here is quite in character. Birling, on the other hand, adopts a sanctimonious and hypocritical attitude when he learns of his son's relationship with Eva.

> **You'd think everybody has to look after everybody else**

Mr Birling expresses his philosophy that **'a man has to mind his own business and look after himself and his own'**. The events of the play show this to be unworkable. Immediately, one of the 'cranks' whom Birling has just been sneering at arrives: Inspector Goole. In fact, the bell rings when Birling is in mid sentence, something that Sheila considers significant in Act 3. It appears later as if the Inspector must have **deliberately** **timed** **his** **entrance** to make it even clearer where his message is aimed.

Birling is still a magistrate, and he and Gerald joke that the Inspector's visit may be about a warrant – that is, unless Eric has been up to something! Eric does not share the joke. He attracts attention, and then suspicion, by his **evident** **alarm** at the news of the Inspector's visit. This clever touch by Priestley alerts us to the possibility that Eric has **something** **to** **hide**.

Inspector Goole has come about a young woman who has swallowed disinfectant to kill herself. The Inspector knows a lot about her because she left a letter and a sort of diary which reveal that she used more than one name. Her original name was Eva Smith, and she used to be employed in Mr Birling's factory.

❝He speaks carefully, weightily ❞

The Inspector makes an **immediate** **impact**. Remember that we have been told in the opening scene directions that the **lighting** is to change at this point. Why does Priestley want the 'pink and intimate' lighting to change now?

Birling rapidly becomes impatient with the Inspector. Notice how Gerald and Birling are not at first worried by his visit. They regard the police as their protectors, but also as their **servants**. This is why, later on, Mr and Mrs Birling take such sharp exception to the way the Inspector speaks to them.

Birling stares hard and with recognition at a photograph of Eva Smith that is shown to him. He recollects, after prompting from the Inspector, that the girl left his factory about two years previously, at the end of September 1910. He can see no connection between this and the girl's suicide, but the Inspector seems doubtful about this.

> **Any particular reason why I shouldn't see this girl's photograph, Inspector?**

Explore

Use of the photograph is one of the Inspector's successful investigative techniques. Which other ones does he use?

Gerald is irritated that the Inspector refuses to let him see the photograph. The Inspector says that he likes to work this way: 'One person and one line of inquiry at a time'. At the end of the play Gerald realises that, by never allowing two people to see the photograph at the same time, the Inspector may have used several different photographs. This is an example of Priestley's dramatic skill.

Why does Gerald say: 'Look here, sir. Wouldn't you rather I was out of this'? Is it just good manners on his part? If it is, why is this kind of behaviour 'good' manners? Or is it that Gerald thinks that there may be some scandal? If so, what could be his motive for not wishing to hear about it?

> **I can't accept any responsibility**

Mr Birling says that his link with Eva can have nothing to do with her suicide, but accepts that it might have been part of 'a chain of events'. He then contradicts this by going on to say that he cannot be held at all responsible for the fate of the girl. Priestley's main argument in the play is that people must accept responsibility for others, whether they like it or not. As Birling points out, this would make life 'very awkward' for some.

> **As you were saying, Dad, a man has to look after himself**

Explore

Where else does Eric challenge the views of his father?

Eric reminds his father of his advice that a man should 'mind his own business and look after himself and his own'. In the light of the Inspector's news about the girl's death, this reminder is embarrassing for Birling. It is the first of many embarrassments which he and others will have to suffer, as they come face-to-face with the truth.

❝Did you say 'Why?'❞

Birling takes exception to the Inspector's tone when he asks why Birling refused to give the workers higher wages, but his objections are swept aside as the line of questioning continues. The characters seem so fascinated by the Inspector's revelations that they do not at first notice the unusual way in which he speaks to them. Inspector Goole not only asks questions, but also comments on the behaviour and attitudes of everyone and passes judgement in a way which a real police inspector almost certainly would not do. Here, for example, he goes on to agree with Eric that the girl could not simply have gone off and worked somewhere else, as Birling suggests.

Explore

Agatha Christie's murder mysteries were very popular at the time the play was written. Read one to see other detection methods at work

Mr Birling recalls that the girl was one of four or five ringleaders in an unsuccessful strike for more money; she was sacked after the strike failed. The Inspector annoys Birling by asking why he sacked her, and Eric sides with the girl, implying that her dismissal was harsh, although Gerald thinks that Birling was right. Here we are beginning to see characters grouping with and against each other. The Inspector hints at secrets yet to be revealed.

❝Well, it's my duty to keep costs down❞

Birling sees himself as a hard-headed, no-nonsense employer. His workers are paid the going rate, no less and no more. He is determined to protect his own interests and those of others like him. His attitude towards strikers is <u>unsympathetic</u>. Those he sees as trouble-makers are given the sack. He has <u>no regrets</u> about what he did to the girl, and is offended by the Inspector's attitude. Eric expresses faint reservations, but his father rounds on him forcefully and tells him to keep out of it.

> *She'd had a lot to say – far too much – so she had to go*

Birling's comments on the sacking of Eva are ironic. He does not see that the words could herald his own downfall, for <u>he too has had a lot to say</u>. Remember that it was while he was saying a great deal to Gerald and Eric that the Inspector arrived.

Eric consistently takes the opposite line to Gerald: '<u>He could. He could have kept her.</u>' Mr Birling finds this increasingly irritating. Notice how Priestley has made the <u>voice of conscience</u> come, appropriately, from <u>inside the family</u>, not from the outsider, Gerald. Is there anybody else in the play who acts as a kind of 'conscience' for the others?

Birling continues to be offended by the Inspector's intrusion. He is proud of being 'somebody' in the local community. It is at this stage that he refers to his friendship with Chief Constable Roberts. Do you think that all the prominent people they mention would be as ready to draw attention to their friendship with the Birlings?

> *No, I've never wanted to play*

Explore

Can you find other occasions when the Inspector uses a word with a different shade of meaning from the other characters?

The Inspector's deliberate misunderstanding of Eric's comment about Eva provides a lighter moment, although it is a weak joke. This provides a contrast to the serious revelations that follow. Do you think the Inspector is making fun of Eric, or does he think that Eric's expression of sympathy is insincere?

This tellingly ironic remark to Eric illustrates Birling's <u>hypocrisy</u>. Just a few moments before, Birling denied any responsibility for the girl's fate. Throughout the play, he is increasingly desperate to avoid facing 'a few responsibilities'.

Sheila returns, not knowing that the Inspector is there. Birling becomes annoyed when the Inspector tells her about the suicide. The Inspector explains how, after being sacked by Mr Birling, the girl remained unemployed for two months before she ran out of money, lost her lodgings and, with no one to help her, became desperate. She then had a stroke of luck and got a job at Millwards, a well-known local department store. After a couple of enjoyable months the girl was told she would have to leave, as a customer had complained about her. Sheila becomes agitated at the mention of Milwards. When the Inspector shows her a photograph of the girl, she runs from the room in distress followed by Birling.

Sheila learns that Eva was 24, which is about the same age as herself. This physical <u>similarity</u> – they are also both described as 'pretty' – draws our attention to their <u>very different</u> <u>lifestyles</u> <u>and</u> <u>fates</u>.

The Inspector makes it clear that we ought to suspect that Gerald, Eric and Sheila do in fact know something: <u>'Are</u> <u>you</u> <u>sure</u> <u>you</u> <u>don't</u> <u>know?'</u> This device of <u>guilt</u> <u>by</u> <u>implication</u> increases the <u>dramatic tension</u>, and leads us to anticipate more links in the chain of events.

This makes a difference

Birling changes his attitude when he is told that the Inspector has come to question everybody. Notice how Gerald has just pointed out that it is what happened to the girl after she left Birling's works which is important. Do you think that Birling feels that he is now off the hook?

Nevertheless, he does not want his daughter involved. He wants to talk to the Inspector 'quietly in a corner', which suggests underhand dealings. He is used to getting his own way, particularly with people that he sees as below him socially.

Immediately she learns about Eva Smith's dismissal from Mr Birling's factory, Sheila is critical of her father: 'I think it was a mean thing to do.' Throughout the play she consistently acts as the family's conscience and is a supporter of the Inspector. To some extent she is helped in this role by Eric, although he is a much weaker and more evasive character than she is.

Why do you think Priestley chose Sheila to fulfil this role? The likenesses between Sheila and Eva increase our sympathy for Eva by suggesting the happier life she might have had. Sheila perhaps speaks on behalf of the dead girl when she accuses the others of indifference, callousness and so on. The fact that the dead girl made none of these accusations herself while she was alive serves to add more weight to Sheila's attacks.

> **"There are a lot of young women living that sort of existence"**

The Inspector's pronouncements are not confined to the Birlings. They apply to society as a whole. We have to look beyond the secure environment of the Birlings' dining room. Priestley achieves this by such statements as: 'it would do us all a bit of good if sometimes we tried to put ourselves in the place of these young women…'. The scope of the play relates to us all. The Inspector's comments are often addressed as much to the audience as to those on stage, and in some productions this is made very obvious by the Inspector coming to the front of the stage to deliver his lines.

And then she got herself into trouble

Explore

Are the Birlings overprotective? In what ways do they try to shield their children from real life elsewhere in the play?

Birling's choice of words is revealing. To what extent is it fair to say that on each occasion Eva Smith met up with one of the play's characters, she '<u>got</u> <u>herself</u> <u>into</u> <u>trouble</u>'? Note how both Birlings try to **cocoon** their children from harsh experiences: 'Why the devil do you want to go upsetting the child like that?' Sheila, in her twenties, is no longer a 'child', just as Eric is not a 'boy.'

The Inspector makes it clear that his purpose is to establish exactly who it is that has made 'a nasty mess' of Eva Smith's life. Notice that he does not spare the Birlings any of the harsh images of the suicide victim. Compare this with Birling's attitude. Why exactly is Birling so upset?

At this point, Gerald asks to see the photograph. Interestingly, although the Inspector says that he may see it later ('all in good time'), Gerald never actually does see it. How different might the rest of the play have been if Gerald had seen the photograph at this point?

When Eric says he would like to go to bed, the Inspector advises him against it on the grounds that he may have to get up again soon. Gerald protests that they are respectable citizens, not criminals. The Inspector says that sometimes he cannot tell the difference.

Sometimes there isn't as much difference as you think

The Inspector returns to this key point throughout the play. It is his central message. He wishes to point out to the characters, and to the audience, the real nature of responsibility

for others. He suggests that the <u>line between guilt and innocence is narrower than is commonly assumed</u>. Sometimes it is hard to establish on which side of the line people find themselves.

Sheila returns. She has told her father that she was the customer who complained. She felt bad about the incident at the time and feels worse about it now. The Inspector says that, like her father, Sheila is only partly responsible for the girl's fate. Sheila explains that the girl, who was attractive, held a dress up against herself in the shop and it was obvious that it suited her. When Sheila tried on the same dress, it didn't suit her and she caught sight of the girl smiling at the other assistant, as if to say that Sheila looked awful. Sheila complained to the manager, saying that the girl had been impertinent. She admits that she was jealous of the girl, but had never done anything like that before.

❝You knew it was me...❞

Sheila is the first to recognise that the Inspector seems to know about them all. Apart from Sheila and Eric, all the characters continue to see Inspector Goole as a police officer or, at the end of the play, as a hoaxer. Sheila is increasingly convinced that he is nothing of the kind, and that his strangeness cannot be explained except in 'other-worldly' terms.

❝So I'm really responsible❞

Sheila is readier than any of the others to <u>admit her guilt and express regret</u> for her actions. The Inspector makes sure that she knows she was only partly to blame. Contrast Sheila's honest admission with her mother's <u>confession</u> at the end of Act 2.

Sheila had insisted on trying on a particular dress, even though her mother and the assistant had advised against it, which suggests a **stubborn** **streak**: 'I was furious with her. I'd been in a bad temper anyhow.' In the event, they had been right; the dress simply did not suit her and she 'looked silly in the thing'. It is clear that being shown to be wrong about the dress put Sheila in a bad mood and she subsequently took this out on the girl.

Compare the different ways in which Eva Smith and Sheila Birling were treated. Eva's activities caused her to be dismissed by Mr Birling and the shop owners. Sheila's actions were clearly much more those of a genuine trouble-maker, but she was **immune** from punishment because of her social position.

Sheila **abused** **her** **power** in much the same way as her father did when he dismissed the girl from his factory. Between them, Sheila and her father deprived the girl of her **livelihood**. The next two Acts show how the other characters contributed to the girl's **spiritual, moral and physical ruin**.

> **How could I know what would happen afterwards?**

Although Sheila says that her actions did not seem to be very terrible at the time, she is the **first to confess** her part in the girl's fate. Notice how she immediately expresses **regret** for what she did and makes only a minimal effort to excuse her behaviour. In this she differs from most of the others. Sheila is also the first, at the end of the play, to **protest** against the way her parents try to pretend that everything is normal again.

> **I'm not going until I know all that happened**

The Inspector performs the functions of **questioner** and **storyteller** in the play. He provides us with the outline of the girl's history, **fills in the background** where appropriate, **recaps** events so far and sometimes, as here, seems to speak for the audience: 'Well, we'll try to understand why it had to happen. And that's why I'm here.'

The Inspector tells them that, after this, the girl changed her name to Daisy Renton. At this, Gerald becomes agitated and gets himself another drink. When the Inspector leaves the room to find Birling, Gerald admits to Sheila that he knew Daisy Renton. Sheila realises that this explains his absence the previous summer. Gerald says he has not seen the girl for six months. He wants to keep this from the Inspector, but Sheila says that is impossible, because 'he knows'.

Explore

What use does Priestley make of entrances and exits in the play?

At this point, Priestley cleverly clears the stage of everyone except Sheila and Gerald, as the Inspector goes with Eric to find Mr Birling.

❝Oh don't be stupid. We haven't much time.❞

Sheila confronts Gerald with his dishonesty just as the Inspector would have done, even echoing the Inspector's urgency: 'we haven't much time'. In spite of Gerald's reluctance to reply, her barrage of questions seems to answer itself. Like the Inspector, she knows. Her refusal to help Gerald cover up events signals the rift between them. After her own confession, Sheila repeatedly seems to be assisting the Inspector.

When the Inspector returns, his simple, 'Well?', leaves the audience in tense anticipation as the curtain falls on Act 1. It is a cliffhanger, which is entirely in keeping with a crime drama.

Text commentary (side margin)

Who? What? Why? When? Where? How?

1   Who expresses condemnation of Birling's dismissal of Eva?

2   Who makes the longest speeches in the Act?

3   What position of importance has Birling held?

4   What is the connection between Birling and Gerald's father?

5   Why does the Inspector refuse a drink?

6   Why was Eva homeless?

7   When is Eva dismissed from Birling and Co?

8   Where does Eva find work after her dismissal?

9   How does Eva die?

10   How does Sheila react at first to the news of Eva's death?

Who is this?

1   'in his fifties, dressed in a plain darkish suit…speaks carefully, weightily, and has a disconcerting habit of looking hard at the person he addresses before actually speaking'

2   'a heavy-looking, rather portentous man in his middle fifties'

3   'not quite at ease, half-shy, half-assertive'

4   'very pleased with life'

5   'very much the easy, well-bred young man-about-town'

6   'a rather cold woman'

Hidden agendas

Every member of the Birling family (and Gerald, about to marry into it) has something to hide, whether or not he or she realises it. Eric is the most aware of his guilty conscience from the beginning of the play, although his secret is the last to be revealed. Can you find five examples in this Act of his restlessness and lack of concentration which reveal this?

Text commentary

Act 2

> *The scene and situation are exactly as they were at the end of Act 1*

Explore

What does the play gain by all the action taking place in the same setting? Research the unity of place in the play.

Some productions of *An Inspector Calls* are played without an interval, so that the action is continuous, as it is for the Birlings.

The Inspector looks at Gerald and repeats his question: 'Well?' Gerald sees that he is to be questioned, and tries to get Sheila to leave the room. She refuses.

> *She's obviously had about as much as she can stand*

Notice how Gerald echoes Mr Birling's <u>concern</u> <u>to</u> <u>keep</u> <u>Sheila</u> <u>away</u> <u>from</u> <u>anything</u> <u>'unpleasant'</u>. Is this because he cares for her and does not wish to upset her? Is it because he thinks of himself as her 'older and better', and is being condescending? Does Gerald still feel that his engagement can be saved if Sheila does not learn too much about his affair with Daisy Renton? His view that <u>'She's</u> <u>had</u> <u>a</u> <u>long,</u> <u>exciting</u> <u>and</u> <u>tiring</u> <u>day'</u> is along the same lines as the patronising remarks of Mrs Birling in Act 3: 'They're overtired.'

One characteristic of the Inspector's questioning technique is to <u>turn</u> <u>each</u> <u>character's</u> <u>words</u> <u>and</u> <u>actions</u> <u>back</u> upon him or her. Here, he draws attention to Gerald's hypocrisy regarding women: 'And you think young women ought to be protected against unpleasant and disturbing things?' This theme of <u>reversal</u>, of revealing <u>the</u> <u>opposite</u> <u>side</u>, and of worlds turned upside down, runs through the structure of the play.

"So that's what you think I'm really like"

Gerald accuses Sheila of wanting to stay so she can see him 'put throught it' by the Inspector. He then protests that he was not implying that Sheila was being selfish or vindictive. Do you believe him? In fact, Sheila **accuses** **herself** of these things, probably because she has been made to recognise that these are her failings. Is it her intention to take pleasure in watching Gerald be 'put through it', do you think? Is this why she says that **'it** **might** **be** **better'** for her to stay?

"If there's nothing else, we'll have to share our guilt"

The Inspector makes another unpoliceman-like comment here. He implies that people should share their innocence and love, but if neither is present, they must share whatever characteristics they do possess. At the end of the play, Sheila and Eric share an attitude that divides them from the others.

There is something else implied in the Inspector's comment. The society in which the Birlings live shares out **material** **riches** very unequally. This is made plain at several points. Although some people, like the Birlings and Gerald, have been granted the lion's share of material wealth, they are reluctant to accept a similar-sized share of **responsibility** for those who have been less generously treated. The Inspector points out that, if this is the case, all that remains to be shared is guilt and blame.

The Inspector's message would have seemed **appropriate** **to** **post-war** **audiences**, concerned about what kind of a world they should be striving for in the future. The central question of the play is whether Eva Smith's fate was mainly a result of the kind of society that existed in 1912, or simply a result of unchanging human nature.

> **He regards her calmly while she stares at him wonderingly and dubiously**

Some kind of **rapport** or understanding now exists between the Inspector and Sheila. From this point she is far more **attuned** to his message and intentions. This is an example of how Priestley **involves the audience** with characters' feelings and thoughts, and encourages us to identify more with some characters than with others, taking sides in their arguments.

Mrs Birling enters, her brisk self-confidence quite at odds with the atmosphere. Sheila tries repeatedly to get her to drop her inappropriate 'society' manner but Mrs Birling accuses the Inspector of being impertinent.

> **I feel you're beginning all wrong**

Sheila tries to warn her mother that the more she puts on **airs and graces**, the worse it will be for her eventually: **'You mustn't try to build up a kind of wall between us and that girl.'** Do you believe Mrs Birling when she says that she does not know what her daughter is talking about? The Inspector comments that 'young ones' are more impressionable, implying that Mrs Birling's attitudes are too **ingrained** to be changed. When the cycle of events begins all over again, at the end of Act 3, will Mrs Birling take the opportunity to begin in the right way?

Sheila is beginning to see through her mother's **facade** of respectability. Mrs Birling **condemns herself** simply by the words she uses. For example, consider her repeated use of 'impertinent'. She ignores Sheila's warnings and persists in trying to use her **social position to intimidate** the Inspector. She has already attempted to discredit Eva as one of the **'girls of that class'**. Her attitude to anyone she sees as beneath her is highly condescending.

Mrs Birling makes two quite untrue statements about Eric – that he isn't used to drinking and that he is only a boy. It is the signal for the **shattering of her illusions**.

She becomes upset when Sheila points out that Eric has been drinking too much for the past two years. Gerald says he has gathered that Eric drinks 'pretty hard'. Birling now enters without Eric.

> **"** *Eric...seems to be in an excitable, silly mood* **"**

Eric is described in language which suggests that he is much younger than his early twenties. The word **'silly'** is the key adjective used in connection with him. It alerts us to the identity of the father of Eva's baby, who is also described as 'silly'.

Mrs Birling is put out because Sheila, not the Inspector, reveals all the embarrassing truths. Although we sense that the Inspector knows a lot more than he pretends, his usual method is to put characters in a position where they have **no choice but to admit the truth** about themselves.

> **"** *He must wait his turn* **"**

The Inspector is **beginning to take over**. Notice how he crosses Mr Birling's instructions that Eric should go to bed: 'He must wait his turn.' He is determined to run the investigation on his own terms and to his own schedule. Both Sheila and Eric now begin to pay more attention to the Inspector than to their own parents. Why do they behave in this way?

The Inspector questions Gerald, who confesses that he knew Daisy Renton. They met first in a bar and then again two nights later. Gerald insisted that the girl used his friend's temporarily available rooms, and gave her money. He makes it clear that he did this without asking for anything in return, but admits that eventually they became lovers. The suggestion is that neither really loved the other: she was grateful, while he was flattered. Sheila is sharply critical of Gerald, but acknowledges his honesty. Gerald explains that the affair ended at the start of September. According to the Inspector, the girl's diary reveals that she went to a seaside place for about two months, feeling that she would never be as happy again. The Inspector allows Gerald, who says he is more upset than he may appear, to go for a walk.

" Then I noticed a girl who looked quite different "

Explore

Does Gerald think of himself as a hero? What language does Sheila use to describe Gerald which continues this theme?

What was Gerald doing in a bar which, as he admits himself, is a known haunt of prostitutes and their clients? Is this another example of his hypocrisy? Gerald describes his behaviour in snatching the girl away from Alderman Joe Meggarty as though he were conducting a rescue mission. Given the way he subsequently used and then discarded her when she became inconvenient, how different do you think Gerald and Joe Meggarty really are?

" We are learning something tonight "

Explore

Mrs Birling's 'learning' is a theme throughout the play. She is learning facts, but how much of a moral lesson is she learning?

Mrs Birling appears shocked to learn of the commonly accepted truth about Joe Meggarty. Is it credible that she can have been so ignorant of his reputation if at least three of the six people present thought it common knowledge?

One of the mainstays of the Birlings' snobbery is that they mix exclusively with people like themselves. As the play progresses, the most respectable members of the local community are thoroughly discredited. What does this imply about the basic values of a society in which such people rise to positions of importance?

People like the Birlings have **pretensions to superiority**, which is not just a matter of wealth, but also embraces moral and social values. Mrs Birling's attitude towards the Eva Smiths of this world ('girls of that class') shows that she thinks herself a **better human being** than they, not merely wealthier.

The play is set in an age when very **high standards** were expected from public figures. Even today we expect public figures to live by higher standards than ordinary people. Do you think this is hypocritical? Think about your feelings towards the characters. Are you glad when it looks as though Gerald and Mr and Mrs Birling are going to get their comeuppance? Do you find the behaviour of Joe Meggarty any more offensive than Eric's, or Gerald's?

> **❝❝*I became at once the most important person in her life*❞❞**

Gerald tells his story at considerable length, giving us many details of Eva's background. The few interruptions are dramatically necessary, to avoid his speech becoming simply a very long monologue. The girl's account of the factory and the shop were, Gerald says, '**deliberately vague**'. This vagueness helps the characters to persuade themselves later that several different girls were involved, although this question remains open.

Gerald says Eva felt '**grateful**', and that it was only natural under the circumstances that they should become lovers. To what extent do you feel Eva Smith was **responsible for her own tragedy**? After all, she did not have to go on strike, any more than she had to accept Gerald's offer of rooms, or go to the Palace bar, or let Eric take her home. Is this a fair attitude to adopt towards Eva?

Although Gerald says that he 'didn't ask for anything in return' for helping Eva, he **failed to think ahead** when they did become lovers. He knew that his friend would want his rooms back after six months, so what would happen to Eva then? He did not consider the possibility that she might become emotionally involved with him. Gerald is in charge of the timing of events here, just as the Inspector is in charge of the timing of the investigation.

Mr Birling says he dislikes the fact that his daughter, 'a young unmarried girl', is being dragged into the affair. His hypocrisy is staggering. His description of his own daughter perfectly describes Eva Smith, but he adopts entirely different standards when considering Sheila.

Both Birling and Gerald have completely different standards for women of different classes. In Act 1, they joke about the 'fun' that young men get up to. Their amusement comes from a boys-will-be-boys attitude to sexual relationships. Gerald uses the girl, then discards her, just as Birling did. Eric uses the girl for sex and treats her, as the Inspector says in Act 3, 'as if she was an animal, a thing, not a person'. What does this tell you about the society in which Priestley sets his play?

❝ I think you'd better take this with you ❞

Sheila refuses to be treated like a child any longer. She rebels against her father's attempt to cut her out of the conversation. Her sharp, inquisitive tone forces Gerald to admit the truth to himself. The process is shown as painful but necessary: as Sheila says, 'I've a right to know.' The suggestion is that each of us has a similar right to know the truth about ourselves. Gerald owes it to himself to tell the truth.

Explore

Why was Gerald expecting the ring back? Is he ashamed of what he has done?

Sheila returns the ring to Gerald, who says that he was expecting this. Sheila tells him that although she now respects him more than she did, they will have to start getting to know each other again, because they have become different people: 'I don't dislike you as I did half an hour ago.'

Sheila is scrupulously fair. Notice how she gives Gerald credit for his honesty and accepts that he acted from honorable motives when he first became involved with the girl. She even accepts partial blame for reducing Eva to the state she was in when she met Gerald. She does not say that she is dropping Gerald for good, merely that they are not the same people who sat down to dinner earlier and that they will have to 'start all over again'.

Gerald goes out for a walk. Do you think the Inspector makes much of an impression on him? He does not appear again until the second half of Act 3. During his absence, certain things about the Birlings are revealed which they are keen to keep hidden when he returns. This technique of making revelations in a character's absence is used several times to develop the story.

Explore

Design a tension graph to show the different moods in the play. This technique provides a good visual aid for understanding the play's structure.

The structure of *An Inspector Calls* is very well crafted to maintain the audience's attention and anticipation. There is much use of contrasting moods: the comfortable self-satisfaction of the characters at the opening turns to anxiety, then terror. They sink partially back into complacency as they are offered an escape route – everything has been a hoax – before their security is suddenly undermined again in the final few seconds.

The Inspector shows a photograph of the girl to Mrs Birling, who claims not to recognise her. The Inspector accuses her of lying and Birling angrily demands an apology. Sheila realises that her mother recognises the girl and tells her parents that they are only making things worse by pretending. The front door slams. Eric has left the house, but the Inspector warns us that he will be needed soon.

❝[massively]: *Public men, Mr Birling, have responsibilities as well as privileges***❞**

Mr Birling's response to the above comment is critical: 'Possibly. But you weren't asked to come here to talk to me about my

Explore

This is not the first time the word 'massively' is used for the Inspector's speech. What does it mean? How do you think he is meant to say these words?

responsibilities.' Sheila's comment, '…I'm beginning to wonder', foreshadows her later remarks about the Inspector and his purpose.

This prefaces a long speech by Sheila, spelling out what has happened so far. In this respect she is acting, as the Inspector sometimes does, like the <u>Chorus</u> <u>in</u> <u>a</u> <u>Greek</u> <u>tragedy</u>. Do you find these passages realistic? Look closely at Sheila's speech. Note the conversational tone and language.

The Inspector forces Mrs Birling to admit to her part in the girl's suicide, but only after she has <u>lied</u> about knowing her. The Inspector uses the name 'Eva Smith' and Mrs Birling agrees that she had seen her, but that the girl called herself 'Mrs Birling'.

Mrs Birling is Chairwoman of the Brumley Women's Charity Organisation. She saw Eva Smith at a committee meeting two weeks previously, where the girl appealed for help. Mrs Birling admits that because the girl called herself Mrs Birling she was prejudiced against her case. Mrs Birling feels that her conscience is clear: the girl only had herself to blame, she lied about her circumstances, she was not a deserving case. She admits that she used her influence to have Eva's application for help refused.

I didn't like her manner

Mrs Birling had felt that the girl had <u>not</u> <u>been</u> <u>respectful</u> <u>enough</u> towards her. She uses the adverb '<u>impertinently</u>' to describe Eva's borrowing of the name 'Mrs Birling'; she has already described the Inspector's way of speaking as 'impertinent'. Notice how Mrs Birling <u>prides</u> <u>herself</u> <u>on</u> <u>being</u> <u>a</u> <u>good</u> <u>judge</u> <u>of</u> <u>character</u>. She says that it did not take her long to get 'the truth – or some of the truth' out of Eva. But Mrs Birling resents the way the Inspector probes for the truth – or some of it – from the others.

Explore

What does Mrs Birling's use of language tell us about her attitude to others?

Mrs Birling is confident that she can resist the Inspector's questioning. She is convinced that she has done nothing wrong. Does the Inspector manage to dislodge her from this view? Given Mrs Birling's **determined** **opposition**, how does he manage to get her to talk about her part in the affair?

The Inspector reveals that the girl was pregnant. This was why she went to Mrs Birling's committee for help. It is made clear that the father of the child is not Gerald Croft and that Mrs Birling knew the girl was pregnant when she turned her down.

66 *Look here, this wasn't Gerald Croft?* 99

Notice how this **suspicion** **is** **raised** **and** **squashed** **at** **once**. Priestley wants the audience to question the motives of the characters and skilfully prevents us travelling up a blind alley. What **dramatic** **advantage** is there in ruling out Gerald Croft as the father of Eva's child?

66 *Mother, I think it was cruel and vile* 99

Sheila and her father have very different reactions. Sheila denounces the act for what it was, while Birling thinks only of the possible **scandal** if the press should take up the story: '**when** **this** **comes** **out** **at** **the** **inquest,** **it** **isn't** **going** **to** **do** **us** **much** **good**'. He is again thinking of the **family's** **image**. It shows how little he has learned from the evening's revelations.

Mrs Birling uses the same expression the Inspector will use in a moment – she says that she lost '**all** **patience**' with Eva. Ironically, it was the girl who showed tact and delicacy in protecting Eric. Mrs Birling displayed only intolerance and snobbery: '**She** **was** **claiming** **elaborate** **fine** **feelings** **and** **scruples** **that** **were** **simply** **absurd** **in** **a** **girl** **in** **her** position.' It is impossible to feel any sympathy for the older Birlings, but we are encouraged to feel some sympathy for Eric and Sheila.

This simple contrast between generations is made more complex by the inclusion of Gerald. Gerald is a more complicated character than most of the others. His function at different times is to side with the Birlings, to act as a contrast to both 'sides' of the family in some way or other, to represent the 'real' upper class, as opposed to the social climbers, to fill in narrative background about the girl, and to supply plausible-sounding explanations at the end of the play.

Mrs Birling says that because the girl lied about being married, she may well have lied about other things. She places total blame upon the father of the girl's baby.

> ❝Make sure he's compelled to confess in public his responsibility❞

Mrs Birling is as blind to the irony of what she is saying as she has been to everything else: her son's drinking, the behaviour of so-called respectable figures of the community, and the revelations about the 'real' family life which surrounds her. Just as her rejection of the pregnant girl was a death sentence for her grandchild, so here her condemnation of the father is a final judgement upon her own son: 'I blame the young man who was the father of the child.'

She has already said that the young man was 'silly and wild and drinking too much', and refers to him now as 'some drunken young idler'. If the audience were not already aware that Eric must be the next one involved, all these words would spell it out for them. They sum up his presentation in the play.

There is **dramatic** **irony** here, since Mrs Birling still does not know what almost everyone else has worked out. She is **delighted** that she has found someone to blame and feels **triumphant** that she has finally cleared herself and outwitted the Inspector. Just as at the end of the play, Priestley here allows a **false** **sense** **of** **security** to develop, before smashing it to pieces. This is a classic technique of the suspense writer.

> ❝ *I don't believe it. I* won't *believe it. . .*❞

Explore

Does Mrs Birling have any redeeming features? Do you pity her for her blindness or blame her for abusing her social position and hurting others?

Mrs Birling finally realises the truth. Notice how she decides whether or not she will believe something, not on the basis of its truth, but on whether she finds it attractive or plausible. The end of Act 2 reveals her as a fatally flawed woman, unable to cope with the real world.

At the end of the Act, Priestley's dramatic skill is demonstrated by the simple device of the Inspector holding up his hand to **focus** **all** **the** **tension** on the silence, interrupted by the sound of the front door, while both the characters and the audience wait for Eric to enter. The curtain falls on Act 2.

Text commentary

Quick quiz 2

Who? What? Why? When? Where? How?

1 *Who was bothering Eva/Daisy in the Palace bar?*

2 *Who is 'entirely responsible' for Eva's death, according to Mrs Birling?*

3 *What was Eva's reason for approaching the committee of the Brumley Women's Charity Organisation?*

4 *What does Sheila give to Gerald before he leaves?*

5 *Why does Mrs Birling pretend not to recognise Eva's photograph?*

6 *When did Mrs Birling see Eva?*

7 *Where did Eva go after the affair with Gerald?*

8 *How does the Inspector claim to know so much about Eva's life?*

Who says . . . to whom?

1 *'I never take offence.'*

2 *'I think she had only herself to blame.'*

3 *'Why are you saying that to him? You ought to be saying it to me.'*

4 *'I feel you're beginning all wrong.'*

5 *'I – well, I've suddenly realised – taken it in properly – that she's dead.'*

Saying no

Find five examples in this Act of the Inspector directly contradicting one or other of the characters.

Open quotes

The confrontational nature of this Act is demonstrated by the quick-fire speed of much of the dialogue. Complete the following exchanges with this in mind.

1 *MRS BIRLING: 'I don't think we need discuss it.'*

2 *INSPECTOR: 'Were you in love with [Eva]?'*

3 *MRS BIRLING: 'I consider it your duty. And now no doubt you'd like to say good-night.'*

Text commentary

Act 3

Eric knows that everybody else is now aware of his part in things. He is cross that Sheila has told the others about his drinking. Mrs Birling is distressed and Mr Birling feels Sheila has been disloyal. The Inspector wants to hear Eric's side of things.

Explore

How would the play's climax have been changed if the Inspector had dealt earlier with Eric?

Why does Priestley save Eric until last? At first, the Inspector dealt with each character's involvement with Eva Smith in strict chronological order: Birling, then Sheila, then Gerald. The sudden switch of order is deliberate. If you had been the writer of the play, which arrangement do you consider would have produced the best climax?

Sheila is now honest enough to have no hesitation in admitting to Eric that she was the one who told their mother about his drinking. However, she is also fair-minded enough to see that honesty cuts both ways, and she refuses to let Eric escape without his acknowledging that she had protected him for a considerable time: 'I only told her tonight because I knew everything was coming out.' It is a further example of Sheila knowing that the pretences have to stop.

Eric says he met the girl in the Palace bar one night the previous November, when he was drunk. He went home with her, threatening to make a row unless she let him into her lodging, and made love to her, although he remembered nothing about it afterwards. On Mr Birling's instructions, Sheila and her mother leave the room at this point. Eric goes on to tell how he and the girl met several times after this, they made love again, and the girl became pregnant. Although they were both very worried about the pregnancy, Eva refused to marry Eric because he did not love her. Eric gave her money to live on – about 50 pounds in all.

'And you made love again?'

The Inspector's question produces an interesting answer. The girl was 'a good sport' and Eric 'liked her', although he didn't love her 'or anything'. Compare Eric's relationship with the girl to Gerald's. Look at the words used to describe the way the relationships developed from casual acquaintance into something much more intimate. Eric complains that he is being criticised as though he were a child: 'Well, I'm old enough to be married.' Mr Birling's reaction to the news of his son's sexual indiscretions is very different from his reaction to Gerald's. Their parents treat Eric and Sheila as though they were still young children. Eric and Sheila have had expensive educations and the best of everything. What have they lacked? How has this contributed to the way they treated Eva?

The Inspector asks whether Eva wanted to marry Eric. Eric's answer again shows that the girl had the 'fine feelings and scruples' which Mrs Birling denied her in Act 2. In fact, she had a stronger sense of moral responsibility than those who ruined her life and drove her to suicide. She would not marry Eric because she knew that he did not love her. She would not take his money because she suspected that he was stealing it. She did not expose him to his mother because that would have been blackmail.

Mr Birling demands to know where Eric got the money, and it becomes clear that he stole it from his father's office.

Mr Birling suddenly shows a great interest in the precise use of words and in establishing exactly what has gone on: 'What do you mean – not really?' He is outraged by his son's evasion of the accusation of theft. Eric claims that because he meant to put the money back it was not really theft. He is unable to say how he might have returned the money, but Birling sees correctly that this is immaterial anyway.

Text commentary

52

Mrs Birling and Sheila come back. Mr Birling tells them that Eric has admitted that he got the girl pregnant and that he gave her money he had stolen from the office. The Inspector gets Eric to confirm that when the girl realised that the money was stolen, she refused more. She also refused to see him again, and Eric demands to know how the Inspector knew this. Sheila says that the girl told their mother. Eric, near breaking-point, accuses his mother of being the murderer of her own grandchild.

" You're not the kind of father a chap could go to when he's in trouble "

Explore

Think about Eric's problems. In what ways has he been 'spoilt'?

The Birlings are not only <u>callous</u> towards those they perceive to be their social inferiors, they are also <u>inadequate</u> <u>as</u> <u>parents</u>. Birling argues that his son has been spoilt. He is more concerned with covering up Eric's wrongdoings, so there is no <u>scandal</u> and <u>loss</u> <u>of</u> <u>status</u>, rather than understanding his son's behaviour.

" I didn't know – I didn't understand "

Mrs Birling's distressed cries carry little weight with Eric. Her excuse fails to convince, because we have seen already how she stubbornly refuses to see anything which does not fit in with her narrow view of the world. We can see that Eric is correct in his analysis, and that Mrs Birling is expert at ignoring unpleasant facts, even when they are thrust under her nose.

" Each of you helped to kill her "

The Inspector begins his <u>summing-up</u>, as a <u>judge</u> would. In the 'trial' of the various characters, he has acted sometimes as the counsel for the defence, at other times as the counsel for the prosecution. Could the <u>audience</u> be said to play the part of the <u>jury</u>, deciding who is guilty and who is not? In keeping with the '<u>whodunnit</u>' <u>genre</u>, this scene also resembles the gathering of characters to hear the conclusions of the detective before an arrest is made. In this case, there is no arrest and the curtain does not fall after the detective has completed his case.

66 Look, Inspector – I'd give thousands 99

Birling would not pay Eva Smith, a good worker who was about to be promoted to leading operator status, another two shillings and sixpence a week. Now he offers thousands of pounds to put right his mistake. He is behaving **as if money is the answer to all problems** and may save his reputation. He is offering the money at the wrong time (as the Inspector points out) – another example of the emphasis on **timing** in this play.

The Inspector sums up by saying that there are millions and millions of Eva Smiths and John Smiths, 'all intertwined with our lives', and that because people do not live alone they are 'responsible for each other'. Then he leaves. The remaining characters begin to assess the events of the evening.

66 We are responsible for each other 99

Inspector Goole's message is that **a great wrong has been committed**. Although only Eric has committed a crime in the legal sense of the word, the Inspector has forced them all to see that it is not enough simply to behave in a 'proper' way, according to a 'code of manners'. Notice the **biblical** tone of the Inspector's words, when he warns them about '**fire and blood and anguish**'. This is also a direct reference to the First and Second World War. The Inspector's prophecy was intended, by Priestley, to shake post-war audiences out of their growing complacency and remind them of the necessity of being responsible for one another.

66 He walks straight out leaving them staring, subdued and wondering 99

Explore

Look at the depressed state of the four characters on stage. How long does it take each one to regain their confidence?

Notice how the Inspector <u>dramatically</u> <u>leaves</u>, without giving the characters a chance to recover from his words.

Although *An Inspector Calls* begins like a typical detective story or 'whodunnit', it soon becomes clear that this is a very strange 'whodunnit' indeed – because <u>everybody</u> <u>'dunnit'</u>. Like many of its characters and events, the play itself turns out to be very different from what it had seemed at first to be. Priestley uses several traditions of a 'whodunnit': an investigation into a murder, a limited number of suspects, some false trails, a brilliant detective. The audience's enjoyment comes from trying to guess who <u>the guilty party</u> is before the Inspector reveals the answer. In Priestley's drama, however, the circle of guilt widens and each character is drawn into the role of villain, rather than eliminated from suspicion.

In *An Inspector Calls*, actions that characters have not previously seen as wrong are revealed as highly immoral by the Inspector. Birling has treated people as cheap labour; Sheila has made others suffer because of her childish tantrums; Eric has been a thief and a promiscuous liar; Gerald has lied to his fiancée and used a girl for as long as it suited him; and Mrs Birling, Chair of the local charity organisation, has failed to show any charity at all. Each character sees his or her self-justification torn to shreds by the Inspector's questioning.

> ❝*Yes, and you don't realise yet all you've done* ❞

Birling's accusation is levelled at Eric and is <u>ironic</u>: of all the characters who fail to realise what they have really done, Mr and Mrs Birling are the two clearest examples. The Inspector's departure is the signal for <u>recriminations</u> to break out. Significantly, Mr Birling begins this, <u>blaming</u> Eric for everything: <u>'You're the one I blame for this.'</u> He is particularly worried about the <u>'public scandal'</u> which may ensue, showing again his concern about image and status.

Explore

Why does Birling not simply own up? Why do he and his wife hold on to their blinkered view of things?

Sheila is staggered when her father says '<u>it</u> <u>turned</u> <u>out</u> unfortunately, that's <u>all</u>'. Birling's easy dismissal of the night's events leaves her speechless: 'I don't know where to begin.' But where should Sheila begin? Where should any of us begin, in trying to decide what to do about a world in which this kind of thing can happen?

> **You told us that a man has to make his own way, look after himself**

For the second time, Eric reminds his father about his pompous and selfish speech near the start of the play. This makes a **dramatic** **link** **between** **the** **beginning** **and** **the** **end** **of** **the** **play**. It is the completion of Priestley's 'circle', within which the action of the play moves. This speech of Eric's is also used to allow Sheila to begin wondering aloud about the real identity of the Inspector.

> **Was he really a police Inspector?**

Alert as ever, it is Sheila who first voices the doubt that will dominate the rest of the action: was Goole a police inspector? Notice that she and Eric take the position that the question is of no importance now: '<u>It</u> <u>doesn't</u> <u>much</u> <u>matter</u> <u>now, of</u> <u>course.</u>' To Gerald and Mr and Mrs Birling the answer to this question is all that matters.

Birling thinks that it was outrageous of the Inspector to talk to a man of his standing in the way he did: '<u>Then</u> <u>look</u> <u>at</u> <u>the</u> <u>way</u> <u>he</u> <u>talked</u> <u>to</u> <u>me.</u>' Again he lists his public offices. Birling takes it for granted that these honours confer upon him some kind of <u>special</u> <u>status</u> which means that people must talk to him in a respectful and deferential way.

Sheila's comment, '<u>He</u> <u>made</u> <u>us</u> <u>confess</u>', is both accurate and interesting. She is also the one who realises that the

information they gave to the Inspector was largely
known to him already. She is intrigued by the
implications of this.

> ❝ *The fact is, you allowed*
> *yourselves to be bluffed* ❞

Explore

How high would this
point go on your
tension graph?

Birling is the one who is bluffing. Look at the way he
immediately panics when the doorbell rings. Contrast this
with the first time the doorbell rings, in Act 1, when
everyone is entirely relaxed. Birling is relieved that it is just
Gerald returning from his walk. Mrs Birling turns to her husband
for leadership. She tells Eric and Sheila to 'be quiet', as if they
were naughty children. They must let their father decide what to
do. Watch how Mr Birling reacts to this. How misplaced is his
wife's confidence in him?

Mrs Birling is more concerned about the way the Inspector
addressed them than with the truth of what he revealed. She
describes the Inspector's manner as '**extraordinary**', particularly
the '**rude way he spoke to Mr Birling and me**'. As far as she is
concerned, there has been nothing 'extraordinary' about her
own behaviour, or that of her husband, towards Eva Smith.

> ❝ *That man wasn't a police officer* ❞

While he was out, Gerald ran into a police sergeant acquaintance
who reveals that their caller was not a real police officer.
Dramatically, Gerald's revelation is crucial, because it allows
some of the characters to believe they are **off the hook**. In a
sense, this is the acid test of what each has learned. Study
closely what each of them does next.

> ❝ *By Jingo! A fake!* ❞

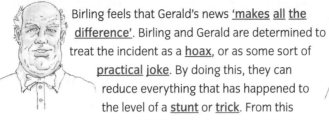

Birling feels that Gerald's news 'makes all the difference'. Birling and Gerald are determined to treat the incident as a hoax, or as some sort of practical joke. By doing this, they can reduce everything that has happened to the level of a stunt or trick. From this point, Gerald and Birling are absolutely united in their attitudes and opinions. Birling addresses him affectionately, 'Good lad!', in contrast to his comments to Eric, who he finds 'damned exasperating'.

Notice how Sheila keeps quiet for the time being, but it must be distressing for her to see her ex-fiancé and father becoming so involved with this clever idea that they lose sight of the real message of the Inspector's visit. The next time she speaks is to say bitterly: 'I suppose we're all nice people now', which only Eric can understand.

Explore

How would you advise the other actors to behave while Birling is on the phone?

Birling telephones the Chief Constable, who confirms that there is no Inspector Goole in the police force. The telephone call is a useful dramatic device. It creates tension, for we only hear one side of the conversation. There are natural pauses, and we have to wait to receive the complete facts. In this case the spelling out of 'Goole' prolongs the wait. Priestley uses phone calls twice more before the end of the play.

> ❝Whoever that chap was, the fact remains that I did what I did❞

Eric has changed considerably during the course of the play, even during the course of this Act. Compare his responsibility and maturity now with the start of the Act when he criticised Sheila for revealing the truth about his drunkenness: 'Why, you little sneak!'

Mr Birling finally loses patience with Sheila's determination to reveal their hypocrisy. It is a sad reflection on Mrs Birling's character that she is more upset by Birling's swearing ('Look – for God's sake!') than by anything she has been told during the evening. The fact that Birling resorts to swearing perhaps indicates that he is beginning to feel undermined by the new Inspector, Sheila.

Gerald suggests that there may not even have been just one girl – perhaps there were several. The Inspector never showed the photograph to more than one person at any one time. Gerald was not shown a photograph at all and had simply admitted to knowing a girl called Daisy Renton. They have only the Inspector's word that this girl was Eva Smith.

❝ *How do you know it's the same girl?* ❞

The Birlings' **desperation** to find a way of **avoiding** **the** **truth** is shown by their willingness to believe Gerald's theory.

If we regard the Inspector as a **hoaxer** (as Gerald and Mr Birling claim) Gerald's theory is highly unlikely. It is a preposterous set of wild coincidences to imagine that different girls got sacked by Birling and Sheila, had affairs with Gerald and Eric and appeared before the charity organisation, all in the correct sequence, and then gave all the relevant information to the hoaxer. The Inspector does not strike the theatre audience as a hoaxer; nor do Eric and Sheila see him that way. If we regard him as some **symbolic** or spiritual figure, then Gerald's theory is perfectly likely, but irrelevant: the potential tragic consequences of their actions have been shown to all the characters.

The idea that up to five different girls might have been involved, one with each of the play's characters, seems incredible, but is it not equally unlikely that five people, all connected with the same family, should each have been involved with the same girl? Although Priestley has constructed his play as though it were realistic, it is in fact more like a **fairy** **story** or **parable** – a story with a hidden moral (a lesson) for us all.

"That doesn't matter to me"

Eric remains **unmoved** by the series of explanations that Gerald and Birling are busy developing. The girl whom he knew is dead; nothing else matters to him.

At this point, Birling surprises the others by asking whether the girl really is dead: *'How do we know she is?'* His question offers the characters **another way out**. Note that Birling's suggestion is written in italics. What clues does this give an actor about how the words should be spoken? Birling convinces himself that it has all been a hoax; there is no one girl, therefore, more importantly, '**No scandal**'. He conveniently forgets that someone might have committed suicide.

Birling is indifferent to the girl's death. If **the fate of 'Eva' can be divided** so that several girls were involved, so much the better. The thought that, if this were true, it would mean that each of the girls suffered injustice, does not worry him. Nor does it occur to him that a pregnant young girl, about the same age as his daughter, died in the infirmary from an agonising suicide. All that concerns Birling is the avoidance of scandal.

Gerald telephones the infirmary. They have not had a suicide for months. Mr and Mrs Birling are delighted, as is Gerald. They are convinced that it has been an elaborate hoax. Eric and Sheila are frightened by the way the others talk.

"Have you had a girl brought in this afternoon...?"

This time it is Gerald who makes a **telephone call** that produces much **nervous tension** in the other characters. He has appeared as a strong and confident character throughout. Notice, however, that even at the end he **tries hard to wriggle out of his** responsibility for the girl's fate. He tries to help Mr and Mrs Birling to do the same. Gerald still hopes to become engaged to Sheila, but sides with the Birlings at the end of the play. Why is this, do you think?

Birling is triumphant: **'The whole story's just a lot of moonshine'**. Before you decide that the whole story is too far-fetched to be true, consider how many real-life events might not be credible if shown in the theatre.

Gerald has been out of the house for a while, to have a 'breather', and has had some time to think. Birling's use of words is revealing: 'He didn't keep you on the run as he did the rest of us.' What sort of person is usually described as **on the run**?

> **❝❝*I remember what he said, how he looked, and what he made me feel*❞❞**

Birling has complacently mimicked the Inspector's words, which 'frightens' Sheila. She **reiterates** his message and **echoes** his threat of 'fire and blood and anguish'. In a traditional 'whodunnit' the criminal would be arrested; here, each 'criminal' must 'remember what he said', must change their ways and must punish themselves by accepting the truth.

Gerald assumes things can now return to where they were before the arrival of the Inspector: 'Everything's all right now, Sheila'. His offer of the engagement ring **echoes** the same event from the start of the play. Another event from the start of the play is about to **repeat** itself. This time, significantly, Sheila refuses him, but she does not turn him away completely. Interestingly, she uses phrases **reminiscent** of the Inspector in her reply, 'not yet' and 'It's too soon', which emphasise the importance of **timing**. Just as Mr Birling accuses Eric and Sheila of not being able to take a joke, the telephone rings.

> **"** *That was the police. A girl has just died –*
> *on her way to the infirmary* **"**

Explore

What effect does this surprising turn of events have on the audience? What might their mood be as they leave the theatre?

The last few seconds of the play provide the <u>final</u> <u>twist</u>. Everyone stares <u>'guiltily</u> <u>and</u> <u>dumbfounded'</u>. It makes a <u>mockery</u> of Mr and Mrs Birling's and Gerald's elaborate self-congratulation. It seems that the older culprits are about to <u>get</u> <u>what</u> <u>they</u> <u>deserve</u>, because they have learned nothing. Should we sympathise with them or be glad that they are not getting away with 'murder'? Will things happen differently this time, when an inspector calls?

Text commentary

Who? What? Why? When? Where? How?

1   Whom does Birling ring to question about the Inspector?

2   Who forgets most quickly the lesson about responsibility the Inspector has taught?

3   What is the Inspector's name?

4   What leads the Birlings to suspect that the Inspector is not all he seems?

5   Why does Gerald return?

6   Why did Eva let Eric into her apartment?

7   Where did Eric meet Eva?

8   How much money did Eric steal?

9   How did he get it?

10   How (according to Birling) will he repay it?

Who says?

1   'I never spoke to her.'

2   'In a way she treated me – as if I were a kid.'

3   'And really, when I come to think of it, why you all had to go letting everything come out like that, beats me.'

4   'Well, he inspected us all right.'

5   'You know, don't you?'

Parallel lines

Where do the following lines in Act 3 find echoes earlier in the play?

1   SHEILA: 'I suppose we're all nice people now.'

2   BIRLING: 'There'll be a public scandal…I was almost certain for a knighthood in the next honours list.'

3   GERALD: (He holds up the ring) 'What about this ring?'

4   BIRLING: 'That was the police. A girl has just died – on her way to the Infirmary – after swallowing some disinfectant, and a Police Inspector is on his way here – to ask some – questions'.

Exams

- To prepare for an exam, you should read the text in full at least twice, preferably three times. You need to know it very well.

- If your text is to be studied for an 'open book' exam, make sure that you take your book with you. However, you should not rely too much on the book – you haven't got time. If you are not allowed to take the text with you, you will need to memorise brief quotations.

- You need to decide fairly swiftly about which question to answer. Choose a question which best allows you to demonstrate your understanding and personal ideas.

- Make sure you understand exactly what the question is asking you to do.

- **Plan** your answer (see page 70.)

- Always have a short introduction giving an overview of the topic. Refer to your plan as you write to ensure you keep on task. Divide your ideas into paragraphs; without them you may not get above a D grade. Try to leave time for a brief conclusion.

- Remember: **point–quotation–comment**: Sheila's engagement to Gerald is short-lived [**point**], because she realises that they are no longer 'the same people who sat down to dinner' [**quotation**]. To call it off is a brave and honest decision [**comment**].

- The key word in writing essays in exams is **timing**. You must know how long you have for each question and stick to this.

- Never forget that you are writing about a play that is meant to be performed, not just read, so consider the effect on the audience in your responses.

- Leave yourself a few minutes to check through your work. It does not look impressive if you misspell the names of characters, settings or the author himself. Remember the second 'e' in Priestley!

- Timing is not so crucial for coursework essays, so this is your chance to show what you can really do without having to write under pressure.

- You can obviously go into far more detail than you are able to in an examination. You should aim for about 1000 words, but your teacher will advise you further.

- If you have a choice of title, make sure you select one that grabs your interest and gives you a lot of opportunity to develop your ideas.

- **Plan** your work (see page 70). Make sure that you often refer to the plan and the title as you write, to check that you are not drifting off course.

- Use quotations frequently but carefully, and try to introduce them smoothly. It is often effective to quote just one or two words.

- Try to state your own opinion with phrases such as 'This suggests to me…'. You will be credited for your ideas as long as you explain why you think them.

- Putting the play in context is very important. Include relevant background detail and explain how the cultural and historical setting affects the writer's choice of language.

- Make sure that you include a short conclusion by summing up your key ideas.

- Don't be tempted to copy large chunks of essays available on the Internet. Your teacher will immediately notice what you have done and will not reward it.

- It is a good idea, if possible, to word process your essay. This will enable you to make changes and improvements to your final draft more easily.

Writing essays

Key quotations

" You're squiffy "

(Sheila to Eric near the beginning of Act 1.) A useful quotation because it shows the typical brother/sister relationship, the colloquial language of the time and an insight into Eric's character. It is also easy to remember!

" I speak as a hard-headed business man "

(Arthur Birling to his family early in Act 1.) This sums up how Mr Birling sees himself and also illustrates his pride. The audience later realises that he is hard-hearted as well.

" Unsinkable, absolutely unsinkable "

(Birling about *The Titanic*, Act 1.) This is an example of dramatic irony, producing a different reaction in the audience from that in his immediate listeners. *The Titanic* could be a metaphor for Birling's own family and prestigious position, which he sees as unsinkable. Most of an iceberg is hidden below the surface, just as the Birlings' – and society's – seediness is hidden below a veneer of respectability.

" We really must stop these silly pretences "

(Sheila to Mrs Birling, Act 2.) This shows that Sheila is grasping the Inspector's message and that a rift is developing between her and her mother. It also highlights a theme of the play – lying.

" Girls of that class "

(Mrs Birling to Sheila and the Inspector, Act 2.) This demonstrates Mrs Birling's feeling of social and therefore moral superiority. She does not attempt to understand an individual case on its own merits. The emphasis is on 'that' and shows how dismissive she is of the working class.

> ❝ *She was very pretty – soft brown hair and big dark eyes* ❞

(Gerald, Act 2.) Gerald's gentle language stresses the contrast between Eva and the usual 'women of the town', who are 'hard-eyed' and 'dough-faced'. This shows that the positive aspects of Eva are always presented to emphasise the negative treatment she receives from others.

> ❝ *We are members of one body. We are responsible for each other* ❞

(The Inspector, Act 3.) This quotation would be essential in a 'message' exam/coursework question. The Inspector's final speech presents the opposite view to the speech Birling made when the doorbell first rang. The message applies to everyone, even the audience.

> ❝ *Everything's all right now, Sheila* ❞

(Gerald to Sheila at the end of the play.) This shows that Gerald has not learned as much as the other younger characters. He is looking at the situation superficially and cannot seem to see that Sheila has changed, even if he has not. He offers Sheila the ring as he speaks, showing his confident and complacent attitude.

1. To what extent is it possible to feel sympathy for Eric?

2. How does Priestley succeed in establishing the characters of the Birlings and Gerald Croft before the arrival of the Inspector?

3. You are Mr Birling at the end of the play. Write your thoughts.

4. How does Priestley make us aware of life outside the Birlings' home and how does this contribute to the message of the play?

5. Sybil and Sheila Birling, mother and daughter, are in some ways like each other, and yet very different. Explore the ways Priestley makes dramatic use of these likenesses and differences in An Inspector Calls.

6. You are the Inspector just after leaving the Birlings' house. Write your thoughts.

7. Who, in your opinion, is most responsible for the death of Eva Smith? Use evidence from the text to justify your opinion.

8. One of the themes of An Inspector Calls is that of lies. Show how Priestley exposes deceit, both in his characters and in society as a whole.

9. The Inspector tells Mrs Birling that the young are usually more impressionable than the old. Is his opinion borne out in the play?

10. You are Eva Smith. Write your diary entry for the day that Gerald finished his affair with you. You could also include your feelings about past events and your plans for the future.

11. Examine how the Inspector is so successful in his methods of investigating the Birlings for their 'crimes' against Eva Smith.

12. How effectively does Priestley convey his social message in An Inspector Calls?

13. Look closely at the end of Act 3 from Gerald's phone call to the Infirmary. How does Priestley make this part of the play so dramatic?

14 Who do you find to be the least sympathetic character in the play? Justify your opinion by close reference to the text.

15 In Act 2 Sheila says: 'I must obviously be a selfish, vindictive creature.' What is your assessment of her character and behaviour?

16 Explore how Priestley uses the conventions of the 'whodunnit' to add tension and excitement to An Inspector Calls.'

17 We never see Eva Smith on stage, but she is vividly shown to us. Examine the different ways in which we learn about her life and personality. What impressions do you have of her character?

18 The Inspector has been called 'the embodiment of a collective conscience'. Examine how he is presented and suggest what impression Priestley might have hoped to leave on an audience when Goole leaves the Birlings in Act 3.

19 'The wonderful Fairy Prince' is how Sheila describes Gerald in Act 2. Explore his character, showing the different aspects that emerge during the play.

20 Eric tells Birling that he is 'not the kind of father a chap could go to when he's in trouble'. How far do you consider that both Birlings have let their children down?

21 By concentrating on two characters, show how Priestley explores the theme of social responsibility in An Inspector Calls.

22 At the end of the play we know that a police inspector is on his way to ask the Birlings some questions. How effective do you find this as an ending? Suggest, using evidence from the text, what may happen this time when an inspector calls.

23 You are Sheila at the end of the play. Write your thoughts about your relationships with your family and with Gerald, and how you think that they will develop in the light of the evening's events.

It is very important to be organised in your approach. Time spent in planning your response will be reflected in the grade you receive.

- The first thing to do is to read the question very carefully to make sure you fully understand it and then highlight key words.

- You will need to make some notes on the topic to help you. This can be done in various ways: a list; subheadings; spidergram; or a mind map.

- The advantage of using a spidergram is that it lets you expand your ideas in a clearly linked, visual way. Put the essay title in the centre of the page. From this a number of key ideas will come out in the form of branches.

- By focusing on each key idea in turn, you will be able to branch out further, as your brain makes connections between the ideas.

- Since a spidergram is a way of charting your knowledge, it is also an excellent revision aid. You could work through a number of essay titles in this way.

- Some people prefer to make a spidergram even more visual, by colour coding ideas and adding pictures or symbols.

- In the planning stage of an essay it is also a good idea to jot down some useful quotations. These need not be lengthy and can be added to your spidergram.

- Each branch of a spidergram might form a separate paragraph in your essay. You can number the branches, so that you are clear about the order of your points. Deal with the main points first.

- Some pupils say that they do not like planning and that they never do so, but the majority of candidates do significantly better when they plan their answers.

To what extent is it possible to feel sympathy for Eric?

upbringing (some sympathy)
- father
  - gives him outer signs of status, e.g. public school, but no life values: 'you've been spoilt' (father's fault)
- mother
  - overprotective: 'He's a boy' (he's in his twenties)

Act 2
- doesn't appear at all
- we hear negative things: 'silly boy', 'excitable queer moods'

relationship with Eva (no sympathy)
- Eva behaves far more honourably than Eric
- shows worst side of Eric
  - 'drunken young idler'
  - 'thief' – but stole because he couldn't confide his troubles in his father
- used Eva 'as if she was an animal, a thing, not a person'

first impressions (very little sympathy)
- immature, silly
- 'squiffy'
- annoying his father

Act 3 (some sympathy)
- turning on his parents, particularly Sybil: 'you killed her...damn you!' (the audience approves!)
- siding with Sheila (a sympathetic character)
- admitting responsibility for actions

Spidergram essay plans

71

Spidergram essay plans

Explore the various ways Priestley makes dramatic use of likenesses and differences between Sybil and Sheila Birling

reaction to news of Eva's death (difference)
important! different attitudes lead to dramatic conflict in Act 2, Sheila tells Sybil she is 'beginning all wrong' with the Inspector

- **Sybil**: told news off stage by Author, this enables Priestley to show her hard-hearted reaction after the news has sunk in: 'girls of that class'.
- **Sheila**: spontaneous shock: 'Oh – how horrible'

attitude to Inspector (difference)
- **Sybil**: antagonistic and haughty, thinks him 'a trifle impertinent', proud that she's the only one to stand up to him
- **Sheila**: co-operative, realises Inspector 'makes you admit to things', supports his views

abusing priviledged position in society (likeness)
- **Sheila as customer at Milwards**: gets Eva sacked, petty jealousy and using family name and status
- **Sybil as chair of charity**: denies Eva help, pride offended/prejudiced, leads directly to Eva's suicide

acceptance of guilt (difference)
- **Sybil**: doesn't accept responsibility: 'I accept no blame for it', only shows distress when her own world is affected (lost grandchild)
- **Sheila**: remorseful: 'I know I'm to blame'

start of play (likeness)
important! need to be seen as similar so that the change in Sheila, and rift between them, is more dramatic

- **seen as united**:
  - both shop at Milwards, ie typical mother/daughter
  - light-hearted dinner table chat

end of play (total rift)
- **Sybil**: resumes complaisant attitude, nothing has changed
- **Sheila**: is willing to change, won't go on as if nothing has happened

72

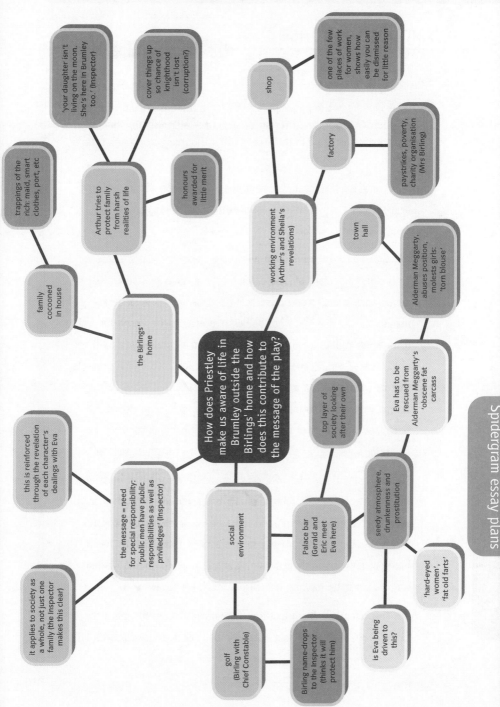

How does Priestley make us aware of life in Brumley outside the Birlings' home and how does this contribute to the message of the play?

the Birlings' home

Arthur tries to protect family from harsh realities of life
- 'your daughter isn't living on the moon. She's here in Brumley too.' (Inspector)
- cover things up so chance of knighthood isn't lost (corruption?)
- honours awarded for little merit

family cocooned in house
- trappings of the rich: maid, smart clothes, port, etc

working environment (Arthur's and Sheila's revelations)

shop
- one of the few places of work for women, shows how easily you can be dismissed for little reason

factory
- paystrikes, poverty, charity organisation (Mrs Birling)

town hall
- Alderman Meggarty, abuses position, molests girls: 'torn blouse'
  - Eva has to be rescued from Alderman Meggarty's 'obscene fat carcass'

social environment

Palace bar (Gerald and Eric meet Eva here)
- top layer of society looking after their own
- seedy atmosphere, drunkenness and prostitution
  - 'hard-eyed women', 'fat old farts'
  - is Eva being driven to this?

golf (Birling with Chief Constable)
- Birling name-drops to the Inspector (thinks it will protect him)

the message = need for special responsibility: 'public men have public responsibilities as well as priviledges' (Inspector)
- this is reinforced through the revelation of each character's dealings with Eva
- it applies to society as a whole, not just one family (the Inspector makes this clear)

Sample response

Look closely at the passage in Act 1 from the entrance of the Inspector to 'Gerald Croft: (*surprised*) Oh – all right'. In what ways does Priestley show in this extract that the Inspector gains total control of the situation?

This extract comes near the start of the play when the Inspector first arrives. I will examine it to show how the Inspector gains control of the situation.

In a way the Inspector has an advantage over Mr Birling because he was not expected. ✔ Inspector Goole is not a policeman that he knows and he does know quite a few because of his work as a magistrate, but this does not bother him at first. The Inspector also gains control because he does not tell them at first why he is there, which makes Mr Birling a little annoyed. It tells you in the brackets that he speaks 'with a touch of impatience'. ✔ This has no effect on the Inspector who just carries on with what he's got to do. At this stage the audience would be interested in the purpose of the Inspector's visit, so in a way he's got control of them as well. ✔

The Inspector does a lot of the talking, which means that he is in more control than the others. ✔ He has some long speeches and even interrupts Mr Birling and makes sure he says what he wants to say. Mr Birling is not used to this sort of treatment. He has a high position in society in Brumley and is used to getting his own way. He's usually the one who says a lot in his family. ✔✔

The Inspector tells them that a young woman died in the infirmary. She'd been taken there that afternoon because she'd swallowed a lot of strong disinfectant. This shocks Eric so that he can only say 'My God!', but Mr Birling says he doesn't see what it's got to do with him.

The Inspector has a photograph and that's one way that he is in control because he doesn't let go of it. He just shows it to Mr Birling and then puts it back in his pocket so that the others can't get a sight of it. ✔ Gerald and Eric want to see it, because they are curious about it. If you have made someone curious about something and only you can give them the answer then you have some control over them. ✔

After that the Inspector gets on with asking Birling some questions and there are interruptions from Eric and Gerald, but the Inspector doesn't let them talk among themselves. ✔ He keeps getting back to the point and ends the extract by telling Gerald, 'I'd prefer you to stay'. So Gerald can't really leave.

Examiner's comments

This is a solid response which shows understanding of the extract and of the Inspector's methods. The candidate demonstrates some insight into how meaning and ideas are conveyed through language, but should focus more on this. Textual evidence is used to support views; however, quotations could be used more frequently and the response could be more exploratory in places. It is rather simplistic and plodding. The essay has a good, clear structure, but no conclusion. The candidate attempts to remain focused on the title, though wastes time at the beginning by repeating the question. Overall, this is an accurate, pleasing, if slightly under-developed response to the question.

Sample response

Look closely at the passage in Act 1 from the entrance of the Inspector to 'Gerald Croft: (*surprised*) Oh – all right'. In what ways does Priestley show in this extract that the Inspector gains total control of the situation?

In this extract we see how quickly the Inspector makes his mark in the Birlings' secure environment. ✓ Until his entrance, Mr Birling has been in control.

In the initial scene directions Priestley instructed that the lighting should become 'brighter and harder' when the Inspector arrives, which gives him a direct advantage, for the family can no longer hide behind the rosy glow. ✓✓

The element of surprise is a form of control by the Inspector. ✓ Initially he behaves like a typical policeman, not drinking on duty and addressing Birling as 'Sir', which might lull Birling into a false sense of confidence. The Inspector's manner soon changes, which is unsettling for Birling. ✓ He answers his questions very briefly, almost verging on impertinence: 'Quite so'; 'No, Mr Birling', leaving Birling at a disadvantage, because he wants more information. ✓ He is becoming rattled, as you can tell from the direction, 'with a touch of impatience'. ✓

The Inspector's speech bluntly giving the facts of Eva's death provokes different reactions from the family, helping Goole to gauge their characters and to work out how best to deal with them. ✓ Birling sees no relevance in the case to him, but the Inspector cuts him off 'massively' in mid sentence (as he did when he rang the doorbell), which suggests his physical dominance. He has Birling 'hooked' ✓

when he mentions Eva Smith's name for the first time, because he recognises it.

The Inspector now introduces one of his main tactical devices – showing the photograph. Only Birling is shown it, although Gerald and Eric would like a look. This is one of the ways in which he gains control over them. ✔ This leads to his other weapon – timing. ✔ He will work on 'one person and one line of enquiry at a time'. Eric and Gerald are unsettled and intrigued, because their turn will come but they have to wait; this also builds audience suspense. ✔

The Inspector's control is shown fully when he does not give Birling a chance to reply to Gerald's suggestion that he leave and gives Gerald no choice but to stay, even though he has no idea what is happening. In that period, people of Gerald's and the Birlings' social position would have seen the police as their servants. ✔ They have done nothing criminal, yet the Inspector is the one giving orders and they have no option but to go along at his pace. ✔✔ They are unused to this and, therefore, at the Inspector's mercy, as are the audience, who are intrigued by his investigation.

> Examiner's comments
> *A well written and clearly organised response from a strong candidate, with a secure grasp of the material. Insight has consistently been revealed into how meaning and ideas are conveyed through language, and frequent quotation has been used to support views. Awareness of the social context of the play and of the effect of the scene on the audience have been shown.*

Quick quiz answers

Quick quiz 1

Who? What? Why? When? Where? How?

1 Eric and Sheila
2 Birling
3 Lord Mayor (two years ago)
4 They are 'friendly rivals in business'.
5 because he is 'on duty'
6 both her parents were dead and she had no money
7 at the end of September, 1910 (nearly two years before the action of the play)
8 at Milwards
9 She commits suicide by drinking disinfectant.
10 She is distressed, asks if it was an accident and then says: 'Oh, I wish you hadn't told me.'

Who is this?

1 Inspector Goole
2 Arthur Birling
3 Eric Birling
4 Sheila Birling
5 Gerald Croft
6 Sybil Birling

Hidden agendas

1 Near the beginning, Sheila says 'so you be careful' to Gerald, and Eric 'suddenly guffaws'. He is unable to explain this.
2 When the Inspector is announced, Gerald jokes that maybe Eric has been up to something. Eric's reaction is sharp and uneasy.
3 When Gerald and Birling are discussing women's clothes, Eric breaks in eagerly: 'Yes, I remember –', then checks himself.

4 Eric is uneasy with the Inspector, bursting out that he's had enough of the enquiry. He wants to go to bed.
5 Note the clues throughout the Act that Eric is drinking quite heavily (for example, he helps himself to another glass of port). This is another sign that he is worried and feeling guilty.

Quick quiz 2

Who? What? Why? When? Where? How?

1 Alderman Meggarty
2 the father of her unborn child
3 She had no money and, because pregnant, could find no work.
4 the engagement ring
5 She does not wish to be implicated in the girl's suicide.
6 two weeks before the action of the play, at a committee meeting for a Women's Charity
7 to a place by the sea
8 He has her diary.

Who says . . . to whom?

1 the Inspector to Mrs Birling
2 Mrs Birling (about Eva) to Sheila
3 Sheila to Gerald
4 Sheila to her mother
5 Gerald to the Inspector

Saying no

1 MRS BIRLING (of Eric): 'He's only a boy'. INSPECTOR: 'No, he's a young man.'
2 MRS BIRLING: 'I don't understand you, Inspector.' INSPECTOR: 'You mean you don't choose to, Mrs Birling.'

3   MRS BIRLING (angrily): 'I meant what I said.' INSPECTOR: 'You're not telling me the truth.'
4   MRS BIRLING (to Sheila): 'I don't understand you. (To the Inspector) Do you?' INSPECTOR: 'Yes. And she's right.'
5   BIRLING (about Eric's departure): 'He was in one of his excitable queer moods, and even though we don't need him here –' INSPECTOR (cutting in sharply): 'We do need him here.'
6   MRS BIRLING: 'If I prefer not to discuss it any further, you have no power to make me change my mind.' INSPECTOR: 'Yes, I have.'

Open quotes
1   INSPECTOR: 'You have no hope of not discussing it, Mrs Birling.'
2   SHEILA: 'Just what I was going to ask.' BIRLING: (rising, angrily): 'I really must protest –' INSPECTOR: (turning on him sharply): 'Why should you do any protesting?'
3   INSPECTOR 'Not yet. I'm waiting.' MRS BIRLING: 'Waiting for what?' INSPECTOR: 'To do my duty.'

Quick quiz 3
Who? What? Why? When? Where? How?
1   the Chief Constable
2   Mr and Mrs Birling
3   Goole
4   He arrived after Birling's speech about everyone minding his or her own business; his manner: police inspectors 'don't talk like that'.

5   He met a police sergeant on his walk, who swore there was no Inspector Goole in the local force.
6   because he was drunk and threatened to make a row
7   in the Palace bar
8   about 50 pounds
9   from the office; collecting small accounts, he gave the firm's receipt and kept the cash
10   He will work for nothing until every penny is repaid.

Who says?
1   The Inspector (about Eva)
2   Eric (about Eva)
3   Birling (to all his family)
4   Sheila (as to whether the Inspector was 'real')
5   Eric (to all those present)

Parallel lines
1   GERALD: 'You seem to be a nice, well-behaved family' (Act 1).
2   BIRLING: '...So – well – I gather there's a very good chance of a knighthood – so long as we behave ourselves' (Act 1).
3   Gerald gives Sheila the ring early in Act 1 and she returns it in Act 2.
4   Edna: 'Please sir, an inspector's called.' (Act 1).

Page 14, JB Priestley, © Popperfoto/Alamy.Com
Page 20, Scene, © Bettmann/Corbis

Design and illustration © Letts Educational Ltd

ISBN 978 1 84315 314 6

First published 1994
Revised edition 2004
05/060611

Published by Letts Educational Ltd.
An imprint of HarperCollins*Publishers*
77–85 Fulham Palace Road
London W6 8JB

British Library Cataloguing in Publication Data.
A CIP record of this book is available from the British Library.

Cover and text design by Hardlines Ltd., Charlbury, Oxfordshire.
Typeset by Letterpart Ltd., Reigate, Surrey.
Graphic illustration by Beehive Illustration, Cirencester, Gloucestershire.
Commissioned by Cassandra Birmingham
Editorial project management by Vicky Butt

Printed in China